TRANSITION INTO BUSINESS

THE DARLA MOORE SCHOOL OF BUSINESS
University of South Carolina

SHIRLEY KUIPER, EDITOR

Prentice Hall
Upper Saddle River, New Jersey 07458

Library of Congress Cataloging-in-Publication Data
Transition into business / the Darla Moore School of Business
    Shirley Kuiper, editor.
        p.   cm.
    Includes bibliographical references.
    ISBN 0-13-081541-1
    1. Business   I. Kuiper, Shirley.   II. Darla Moore School of Business
    HF1008.T725   1998
    650—dc21   98-39132
                                                                    CIP

Production Supervision: *Kathryn Pavelec Kasturas*
Interior Design and Page Layout: *Kathryn Pavelec Kasturas*
Managing Editor: *Mary Carnis*
Director of Production and Manufacturing: *Bruce Johnson*
Manufacturing Manager: *Marc Bove*
Acquisitions Editor: *Sue Bierman*
Editorial Assistant: *Michelle Williams*
Marketing Manager: *Jeff McIlroy*
Cover Design: *Liz Nemeth*
Cover Illustration: *Nikolai Punin*
Interior Illustrations: *North Market Street Graphics*

©1999 by Prentice-Hall, Inc.
Simon & Schuster / A Viacom Company
Upper Saddle River, New Jersey 07458

Printed in the United States of America

10 9 8 7 6 5 4 3 2 1

ISBN 0-13-081541-1

Prentice-Hall International (UK) Limited, *London*
Prentice-Hall of Australia Pty. Limited, *Sydney*
Prentice-Hall Canada, Inc., *Toronto*
Prentice-Hall Hispanoamericana, S.A., *Mexico*
Prentice-Hall of India Private Limited, *New Delhi*
Prentice-Hall of Japan, Inc., *Tokyo*
Simon & Schuster Asia Pte. Ltd., *Singapore*
Editora Prentice-Hall do Brasil, Ltda., *Rio de Janeiro*

CONTENTS

PREFACE

Transition into Business is intended primarily for use in an orientation or transition course for first-year students who are interested in business. It introduces students to basic business concepts they will encounter repeatedly in their business education and also introduces career options and requirements.

The book is organized around two models, the *Business Function Integration* model and the *Recurring Themes* model, which are introduced in Chapter 1. These models were designed to provide an integrated view of business. The Business Function Integration model reinforces the fact that business success depends on interactions among all functional units. Each unit provides information to and takes information from other units to contribute to the overall success of the company. The Recurring Themes model focuses on fundamental knowledge and skills that penetrate all business studies and all areas of the firm.

In addition to reviewing the content of each chapter, an end-of-chapter Discussion and Action section provides written and oral communication assignments that encourage students to explore their career interests in a variety of ways. Suggested activities include gaining information through interviews, exploration of the World Wide Web, and library searches.

Each chapter was contributed by one or more professors from the academic units in The Darla Moore School of Business at the University of South Carolina or a person in a related academic position in a school of business. The following authors are on the faculty of The Darla Moore School of Business.

- Dr. Jeffrey S. Arpan, Professor of International Business
- Dr. LeRoy D. Brooks, Professor of Finance
- Dr. J. Stanley Fryer, Professor of Management Science
- Dr. Shirley Kuiper, Associate Professor of Management

- Dr. John E. Logan, Associate Professor of Management
- Dr. William H. Phillips, Associate Professor of Economics
- Dr. Terence A. Shimp, Professor of Marketing
- Dr. Ronald P. Wilder, Professor of Economics

Other authors include:

- Mr. James L. Burkett, Lecturer in Accounting, The Darla Moore School of Business
- Ms. Martha W. Thomas, Director of the Center for Business Communication, The Darla Moore School of Business
- Ms. Courtney R. Worsham, Ph.D. Candidate in Marketing, The Darla Moore School of Business
- Dr. Jon M. Werner, Associate Professor of Management, University of Wisconsin at Whitewater
- Dr. Neil W. Sicherman, Associate Professor of Finance, Crummer Graduate School of Business, Rollins College

No attempt was made to change the voice of each writer. As students read the chapters, they should get a sense of the kinds of people they will encounter in their classrooms and the content of the courses they will study.

Several individuals contributed to this book by providing constructive reviews of the manuscript. These reviewers are:

Robert L. Dean, Ph.D., Viterba College
Mary Dubois, DeVRY Institute of Technology-Irving (Dallas)
Donna Loraine, Ph.D., DeVRY Institute of Technology-Kansas City
Robert Reinke, University of South Dakota
James W. Cagley, Ph.D., University of Tulsa
Pamela Perry, University of Arizona

The authors wish you success in assisting students with their transition into business.

BUSINESS FUNCTION INTEGRATION
Functional activity viewed from the perspective of the whole enterprise.

MANAGEMENT ACTIVITY → **Strategy**

Target Product/ Processes

Process/ Management Technologies

Segment Identification, Selection, Exploitation

Product/ Process Design

Product/Service Characteristics

Process/ Product Engineering

Supplier Networking

OPERATIONS

MARKET REQUIREMENTS → **Market Position**

Price? Match? Efficient? Match? Sell?

Invest Cost Cost Invest Cost Revenue Invest Revenue

FINANCIAL ANALYSIS → **Profit**

RECURRING THEMES

COMMUNICATION·TEAMWORK

BUSINESS ENVIRONMENT & ETHICS

ECONOMICS

ACCOUNTING

INTERNATIONAL BUSINESS

BUSINESS

INFORMATION SYSTEMS/COMPUTER APPLICATIONS

ENTREPRENEURSHIP

QUANTITATIVE BUSINESS ANALYSIS

CHAPTER 1

AN INTEGRATED VIEW OF THE FIRM

OBJECTIVES

After you have read this chapter and completed related activities, you should be able to:

1. Identify major functional areas of a business.

2. Explain the importance of integrating information and activities across the functional areas.

3. Identify seven areas of skill and knowledge that are fundamental to all business functions.

4. Give examples of how communication and teamwork influence the success of a company.

The objective of the undergraduate business administration program that you are entering is to provide you with knowledge and skills related to the functional areas of business, communication and teamwork, and other disciplines that are essential to the successful operation of a firm in a competitive, global, highly technological business environment. Wherever you attend school, the business program is designed to build your understanding and appreciation of a successful business enterprise as an integrated entity that depends on many skills and a broad range of knowledge.

Each chapter of *Transition into Business* was contributed by one or more professors with expertise in the area discussed in the chapter. As you read the chapters, you will get a sense of the kinds of people you will encounter in your classrooms, and the content of the courses you will study. The authors wish you success as you embark on your transition into business.

This book is organized around two models, the *Business Function Integration* model and the *Recurring Themes* model. Those models are shown at the beginning of this chapter. The purpose of the models, and of the entire book, is to emphasize two important facts about business:

1. Each unit within a firm has functions and activities for which it is primarily responsible. For example, the accounting unit is responsible primarily for maintaining accurate records and reporting the results of financial transactions, such as sales and the costs of manufacturing, marketing, and distributing the company's products or services. Similarly, the human resources unit is primarily responsible for hiring, developing, and maintaining an adequate workforce and for developing and implementing all policies related to the management of the people employed by the company.

2. A successful firm coordinates the primary responsibilities of the separate units in such a way that the work of all units is integrated and contributes to the overall success of the firm. For example, Marketing cannot promise a new product to a potential customer until it has determined whether Operations can produce the product at an acceptable price, whether Human Resources can supply the necessary workforce to produce and deliver the product, and whether Finance can fund the entire production and marketing effort.

The Business Function Integration model emphasizes the interdependence of the functional units in the organization; the Recurring Themes model emphasizes that the functional units and their employees draw from many areas of knowledge and require many types of skills to achieve success.

BUSINESS FUNCTION INTEGRATION MODEL

The primary functions of Management, Operations, Marketing, and Finance are always essential to a business, but the importance of each unit may vary among different kinds of businesses. For example, a clothes fashion house may view marketing as the key to its success, but it also realizes that adequate attention must be focused on the other three areas if the company is to be successful. Finance may be the predominant functional area in a bank; but if the bank has faulty operations and cannot process transactions efficiently, or if it ignores marketing, it is doomed to fail.

In an effective organization, there is a successful transfer of needed information among the four primary activity centers shown in the Business Function Integration model. The lines between functional area boxes represent required information transfer and analysis among the four functions. The extent of the ties between and among areas of a business represents the level of *integration* achieved within the business. More integrated companies will have ties in greater number, breadth, and quality.

For example, in a small owner-operated business, the functions of management, marketing, operations, and finance are controlled by one person—the owner-entrepreneur. That individual *is* each of the functional units shown in the model. When making decisions about the company, the owner-manager confers with himself or herself as the owner-marketer, owner-producer, and owner-finance officer. As the company grows, the owner-manager may hire a business manager to handle some of the accounting and finance responsibilities and an operations manager to handle the production and distribution responsibilities. But the owner-manager must maintain a constant link with those functions to ensure the success of the business.

RECURRING THEMES MODEL

The success of any business organization, large or small, is dependent on integration of information from much more than the four functional areas highlighted in the Business Function Integration model. The Recurring Themes model contains seven additional areas of information that are used extensively by successful enterprises. A failure to obtain needed information from any of the seven areas—or failure to analyze the information appropriately—will generally lead to poor, or possibly fatal, company performance.

In your business curriculum, you will be exposed to each of the areas presented in the Recurring Themes model. The exact titles given to the themes may vary, but all comprehensive business programs include some instruction in each of the areas. Some schools will offer majors in some of the areas; other schools will offer only one or two courses. Whether you study an area at the introductory level or in depth, you will gain insights into its importance for all business operations. Specifically, your curriculum will include study of:

- *Economics:* how a private enterprise economy functions; the role of producers, consumers, and government agencies in that economy.
- *Business environment and ethics:* the importance of management's sensitivity to the environment in which it functions and its responsibility to a variety of stakeholders.
- *Accounting:* the role of accounting in maintaining accurate records of the firm's activities, analyzing the significance of those activities, and planning for future actions.
- *Information Systems and Computer Applications:* the significance of computer technology as a tool to improve a firm's overall efficiency, including such functions as recordkeeping and analysis, communication, planning, obtaining supplies and materials, production, marketing, and delivery.
- *Quantitative Business Analysis:* how mathematical models and forecasting techniques can improve the effectiveness of all functional units.
- *Entrepreneurship:* the importance of entrepreneurial (creative, risk-taking) thinking in business, whether in a small firm or a large corporation.
- *International Business:* the significance of a global view in all business decisions.

The Recurring Themes model suggests, further, that all elements of business depend on effective communication and teamwork. Today we hear much about cross-functional teams in large corporations. Such teams are composed of employees from different functional areas who work together to enhance product demand and to improve product quality while cutting costs. Whether the company is large or small, effective communication and teamwork are keys to achieving success. They enable better coordination of activities among the four primary functions shown in the Business Function Integration model.

INTEGRATION AND TRANSITION

The models introduced in this chapter emphasize two business realities:

1. A successful firm requires coordination among its diverse functional units.
2. Each unit within a successful firm draws information from many sources.

Therefore, a successful business student will master the information and skills related to the functional areas such as management, marketing, operations, or finance. A successful business student will also master the general knowledge and skills that permeate all areas of business.

Two of those general skills are *communication* and *teamwork*. At both the individual and the company level, communication and teamwork are keys to business success. In Chapter 2 you will be introduced to the importance of business communication and some of its forms and styles. You will also be introduced to communication behaviors that contribute to effective teamwork.

DISCUSSION AND ACTION

1. Look up the following terms in a dictionary of business and economics. In a class discussion, share your current understanding of each term as it relates to the operation of a business.
   - management
   - operations
   - marketing
   - finance
   - accounting
   - economics
   - business environment
   - business ethics
   - management information systems
   - quantitative business analysis
   - entrepreneurship
   - international business
   - communication
   - teamwork

2. Explain in 300 words or less the concept of *integration* among business functions, as presented in the Business Function Integration model.

3. Explain in 300 words or less the concept suggested by the Recurring Themes model.

4. Identify the major functional areas of your college (instruction, administration, maintenance, and so on). Discuss the kinds of coordination that are necessary among those units to achieve a successful educational enterprise. What knowledge and skills from the Recurring Themes model contribute to the coordination of the units' activities?

5. Review your local newspaper or a business magazine such as *Business Week*, *Fortune*, or *Forbes*. Identify one story that illustrates either how effective communication or teamwork contributed to the success of a business or how ineffective communication or teamwork contributed to the failure of a business.

COMMUNICATION·TEAMWORK
COMMUNICATION·TEAMWORK
COMMUNICATION·TEAMWORK

COMMUNICATION

COMMUNICATION·TEAMWORK
COMMUNICATION·TEAMWORK
COMMUNICATION·TEAMWORK

BUSINESS

COMMUNICATION·TEAMWORK
COMMUNICATION·TEAMWORK
COMMUNICATION·TEAMWORK

TEAMWORK

COMMUNICATION·TEAMWORK
COMMUNICATION·TEAMWORK

CHAPTER 2

COMMUNICATION AND TEAMWORK

OBJECTIVES

After you have read this chapter and completed related activities, you should be able to:

1. Explain the importance of communication in business.
2. Plan and develop a letter, memo, or short report.
3. Use appropriate business format for a letter, memo, or short report.
4. Explain why you should become proficient in using a computer as a communication tool.
5. Plan and deliver a brief business presentation.
6. Recognize and practice functional communication behaviors during a group discussion.
7. Recognize and avoid dysfunctional communication behaviors during a group discussion.

In the Recurring Themes model, the themes are superimposed on a background of communication and teamwork, which implies that those activities support all business endeavors. It is not accidental that both communication and teamwork appear to undergird the model. One of the things that business executives repeatedly tell administrators and faculty in schools of business is that schools in the United States are doing a pretty good job of equipping students with the business knowledge and technical skills required to perform on the job. However, their greatest wish is to find more job applicants who possess strong communication skills and are able to function well in work teams. Those two skills are inseparable. Clearly, effective team activity requires effective communication among team members. Moreover, business executives often identify communication skills as the major factor contributing to career advancement.

WHAT IS BUSINESS COMMUNICATION?

It is no exaggeration to say that the single most important activity in business is communication. Businesses depend on communication to plan their strategies; to hire, train, and motivate their employees; to produce and market their products or services; and to report the outcome of their operations. Whenever a company's communication is less than optimal, its operations are less than optimal. In reality, poor communication can lose customers, wreck careers, cause cost overruns, attract bad press, and generally wreak havoc in a business.

Business communication differs from communication in other settings in one major aspect: Its purpose is always to stimulate action. Whether the message is a magazine advertisement, a sales presentation to a prospective customer, a letter to a dissatisfied customer, an instruction manual, a memo containing information about a new employee benefit, or the company's annual report, the ultimate objective is to stimulate the reader to act. Sometimes the resulting actions are overt and even dramatic, such as the 1998 merger of NationsBank and Bank of America. At other times the actions are less dramatic and may even be covert, such as an employee's decision to listen carefully to a coworker's contributions to a team discussion.

The previous examples imply that business communication encompasses a broad range of skills. Those skills include the ability to write efficiently and effectively, to make presentations, and to use the latest computer technology as a communication tool. You should also master the unique skills required to work effectively as a member of a work team.

COMMUNICATION IN THE BUSINESS CURRICULUM

Many business curricula require that students take at least one course that is devoted to business or professional communication. Although the emphasis varies among colleges, the business communication course will tend to build on the writing instruction you receive in your freshman English courses. Some schools also require a basic course in speech communication to complement the business communication course.

Whether a college offers one or more courses in business communication, the instruction often includes business writing, business presentations, use of computers as communication tools, and development of team skills. This chapter gives you a brief preview of those aspects of business communication. You will begin developing your business communication skills in this course, but you should develop them further in specific business communication courses and apply them in all of your business classes.

BUSINESS WRITING

The first thing to understand about business writing is that it differs from other kinds of writing with which you may be familiar. Writers with limited experience typically approach each new writing task with the same set of strategies, expectations, and rules they learned in their high school and freshman English classes. But the rules of effective writing are by no means universal. A business report written for an accounting course will differ significantly from a book report written for an English course or a lab report written for an engineering course. These differences can be best understood as a matter of genre.

You may already be familiar with the term *genre* as it is applied to artistic compositions. We talk about country music versus rock, action films versus romantic comedies, painting versus sculpture, poetry versus fiction. But the concept of genre also applies to the compositions you produce in your course work as well as to the "compositions" business people produce in the workplace: the letters, memorandums, reports, and presentations that constitute business communication.

Genres in writing are distinguished by the purpose and audience of the text (Axelrod and Cooper, 1994). Thus, the character analysis you write about Hamlet for your English class belongs to a genre called a *literary essay*. Its audience are members of an academic community (your teacher and classmates) and its purpose is the illumination of a literary text (the play *Hamlet*). In contrast, the report you write about a member of your work team's job performance belongs to a genre called an *employee evaluation*. Its audience is the management of your company and its purpose is to convey information to assist a manager in taking some action regarding the employee—a raise, a promotion, a warning, or a commendation. These differences in audience and purpose give rise to distinct sets of conventions for each genre.

Conventions are the generally-accepted principles, procedures, and features of a genre. In a literary essay, for example, the conventions include a thesis statement at the beginning of the essay and the use of textual paraphrase or quotations as evidence to support the thesis. In an employee evaluation, the conventions include a standardized set of evaluative measures, a format for presenting those measures, and the use of a writing style that is objective and impersonal. Individual texts can vary widely within a genre, but they still follow the same general conventions. An employee evaluation, for instance, may be positive for one individual and negative for another, but each still is recognizable as an employee evaluation. Similarly, the specific format of the evaluation may vary somewhat from company to company, yet remain within the conventions of the genre.

As a student in your business classes—indeed, in all your classes—you will increase your chances of performing well on written assignments if you take the trouble to first understand the conventions of your genres. Business genres differ from academic genres in a number of ways, as shown in Table 2-1.

Table 2-1
A Comparison of Academic and Business Genres

	Academic Genres	*Business Genres*
Purpose	To create knowledge	To move the audience to action
Audience	Members of the academic community	Targeted decision makers (primary and secondary audiences)
Direction	Horizontal (same field) or cross-channel (different fields)	Upward, downward, horizontal, cross-channel
Style	Usually formal	Formal and informal
Voice	Usually active	Active and passive
Structure	"Argumentative" organization; thesis-based structure; long paragraphs	"Persuasive" organization; direct or indirect structure; short paragraphs
Authorship	Usually individual	Often collaborative
Media	Usually print	Print, visual, oral

An understanding of your genre is just the first step toward effective business writing; there are other steps you should follow as well. Before you begin to write, clarify the purpose of your communication. This is not always as obvious as it sounds. For example, the purpose of a job application letter is not to get the job but to gain an interview for the job. Also be sure to know your audience. In business writing there is frequently more than one audience. The primary audience for your progress report may be your immediate supervisor; secondary audiences may be upper management or other team members at your own level.

An effective technique for learning how to do business writing is imitation. Find good examples of the genres you'll be working with and use them as models for your own writing. In the appendixes to this book you will find examples of business letters, reports, and a memorandum that will introduce you to the most frequently used business communication formats.

Finally, you will become a better writer of every kind of text if you learn how to view writing as a process. Understand that writing consists of several activities: planning, drafting, revising, and proofreading. Don't try to do everything at once. Pace yourself to be able to set aside your writing and come back to it with a fresh perspective. Use a second reader for feedback to help you revise, and use a handbook to identify and correct errors during proofreading. The following list of guidelines should help you improve your writing.

1. *Follow instructions.* Whether in your classes or on the job, be sure to understand any assignment you are asked to do. Identify the genre in which you will be writing and find out the conventions that distinguish it from other genres.

2. *Allow enough time for the writing process.* Planning, drafting, revising, and proofreading are all necessary stages of the process. Give yourself time to fully accomplish each activity.

3. *Organize your text to support your purpose.* Inexperienced writers frequently arrange their text material in the order it occurs to them. A

more effective arrangement takes into consideration the purpose of the writing, the likely response of the audience, and the organizational conventions of the genre.

4. *Use concrete language and specific examples instead of generalizations and abstractions.* In business writing, where the purpose is to stimulate action, it is especially important to be specific about what you want to accomplish.

5. *Use sufficient evidence to support your points and document evidence properly.* Your credibility may be questioned if you do not offer believable evidence to illustrate and support your points. Failure to properly document your evidence leaves you open to accusations of plagiarism.

6. *Remember that grammar matters.* The structural and surface features of language, what we commonly call grammar, are important components of every genre. In written language, particularly the language of the workplace, compliance with grammatical conventions is essential if your work is to be taken seriously.

7. *Don't mistake spellcheck and grammarcheck functions for proofreading.* The spellcheck function in your word processing program can overlook misspellings if the word is a homonym (there/their/they're, to/too/two, witch/which). Moreover, grammarcheck functions will sometimes misdiagnose an error or overcorrect a text that is best left alone. There is no substitute for careful proofreading by a human eye.

The appendixes present examples of appropriate formats for business letters, a memorandum, and reports. A letter is commonly used for written communication with people or organizations outside of the sender's organization. Appendix A demonstrates and explains the block letter format, the most commonly used format for business letters in the United States. Appendix B shows the Simplified Block Letter, a format that is growing in popularity. Appendix C illustrates and explains the standard memorandum format, which is used for written messages within an organization. Appendix D illustrates a report title page, and Appendixes E and F show two formats for business reports that are useful when the report is too long to be contained in a letter or memorandum. As a report increases in length and complexity, you can assist your reader by supplying meaningful headings. Appendix G illustrates levels of headings in reports.

BUSINESS PRESENTATIONS

In addition to writing letters, memos, and reports, you will often communicate by way of a business presentation. A business presentation differs from a public address in three ways: audience size, use of visual aids, and use of a question/answer session. A business presentation is typically given to a relatively small audience, perhaps as small as two or three people and rarely larger than twenty. Most presenters accompany the oral message with visual aids, such as charts, pictures, or computer-projected slides to support the main points of the presentation. Because presentations are intended to stimulate action, a question/answer session allows the audience to clarify issues, and increases the probability that the audience will act as the speaker suggests.

Planning Guides

As you prepare a presentation, apply the following structure to the message:

1. *Create an effective opening.* An effective opening statement has these characteristics:
   - It grabs the attention of the audience.
   - It is related to the presentation topic.
   - It shows the relevance of the topic to the audience.
2. *Give an explicit preview.* Tell the audience where you are going. What points will you cover?
3. *Develop your main points.* Discuss the points in the order in which you gave them in your preview statement. For each point, give enough information (data, examples, anecdotes, etc.) to make the point interesting and convincing. Use visual aids to clarify your information or to add interest.
4. *Use a memorable closing statement.* Ask yourself, "What do I want the audience to do (or remember) as they leave the room?" The closing may be a call for action, a recommendation, or a summary of the main points. It should be clearly related to the opening, providing a sense of closure.

Practice and Delivery Guides

Practice the presentation several times before you appear before your audience. Practice aloud and in front of a mirror, a video camera, or a friend so that you can get feedback about your delivery style. During your practice and as you evaluate the feedback, focus on the physical and vocal aspects of the delivery, as well as the structure and content of the message. An evaluation guide is given in Appendix H. Use it to prepare for and evaluate your presentations.

COMPUTERS AS COMMUNICATION TOOLS

Because every business employee today is expected to use the computer as a standard communication tool, you must become proficient in using the computer to produce effective written documents and business presentations. You must be able to compose, revise, and edit messages at a computer, which means becoming familiar with the features of word processing software and learning to key (type) with ease. You will also be expected to illustrate your oral and written messages with professional graphics and charts; therefore, you must master the use of spreadsheet software that helps you organize quantitative data and design charts. You must also become skilled at using presentation software, with which you can prepare professional verbal, graphic, and pictorial slides to be displayed by computer or overhead projector. In addition, most computers in business offices today are networked, facilitating communication within the organization or around the world. Your employer will expect you to be proficient in the use of e-mail and the Internet for rapid transfer or retrieval of information.

Some computer skills may be taught in a business communication course. In many instances, however, those skills are taught in a computer science, management science, or information systems course. Many schools require students to possess basic computer skills before they enroll in a business communication course so that those skills can be reinforced or expanded in the communication class.

TEAM SKILLS

Another essential communication tool is the ability to work as a team member. Teams function most effectively when members encourage functional communication behaviors and discourage dysfunctional behaviors. Functional behaviors are those that contribute to task performance and team cohesion. Dysfunctional behaviors tend to place excessive emphasis on an individual, thereby distracting others from task accomplishment and team cohesion. Communication theorists Benne and Sheats first proposed the idea of task-oriented, process-oriented, and dysfunctional behaviors in 1948. Since then, many people have benefited by developing the useful behaviors and overcoming the dysfunctional behaviors that are described here.

Task-Oriented Behaviors

Six distinctive behaviors focus on the group's task and help the group accomplish its goals (Table 2-2).

Table 2-2
Task-Oriented Behaviors

Behavior	Example
Initiate discussion	This looks like an interesting project. Let's begin.
Seek information	How many customers returned the completed questionnaire?
Give information	Forty percent of our policyholders are under age 30.
Coordinate	Laura's best customers are recent college graduates, but Mario's sales to that market have been slow. Let's look at their sales strategies.
Evaluate	The major difference seems to be the timing of their calls.
Summarize	Mid-afternoon seems to be the best time to call for an appointment. Does everyone agree?

Process-Oriented behaviors

Five behaviors encourage effective group interaction (Table 2-3).

Table 2-3
Process-Oriented Behaviors

Behavior	Example
Encourage	That's helpful information, Sandy. Have you observed other differences?
Harmonize	Joan, your suggestion for a time-management seminar is good. Could we combine it with Paul's suggestion for a program on telemarketing?
Open gates	Barbara, you seemed ready to say something.
Act as a liaison	I'll get that information from Accounting before our next meeting.
Set standards	We'll start at 9 A.M. tomorrow. Does everyone agree?

Dysfunctional Behaviors

Five actions tend to disrupt group unity and prevent the group from accomplishing its tasks (Table 2-4).

Table 2-4
Dysfunctional Behaviors

Behavior	Example
Blocking	Using criticism or interruptions to prevent the group from reaching agreement.
Seeking recognition	Clowning, bragging, or monopolizing the discussion.
Competing	Expressing different views simply to gain attention or to attack individuals.
Withdrawing	Acting bored and indifferent; refusing to participate or accept responsibilities.
Repeating	Using one or two ideas repeatedly, even after the group has rejected the ideas.

A guide to group roles is shown in Appendix I. Use it to evaluate the behaviors that you and your group members display as you work on a team project.

USING YOUR COMMUNICATION SKILLS IN BUSINESS COURSES

Because executives constantly emphasize the importance of effective communication skills, you should begin developing those skills now. Each chapter in this book contains discussion topics that lend themselves to oral or written communication. Use every opportunity to participate in discussions of those topics and others that arise in your business classes.

Try approaching your course work as if it is your job and the professor is your boss. The employee who assumes responsibility for growth on the job is the most likely to be promoted. If you start assuming responsibility now for your own educational experience, you not only increase the likelihood of earning a good grade, you also prepare yourself to assume the responsibilities that will enhance your career in the future. When you participate in oral discussions, speak articulately and project your voice so that everyone can hear you. Also use class discussions as opportunities to develop the functional communication skills that contribute to effective teamwork. When you are given a written assignment, use the professional business formats that are demonstrated in the appendixes.

Constant reinforcement of the business communication skills discussed in this chapter will place you ahead of students who consider technical business skills to be more important than communication skills. You will be able to demonstrate to your instructors and to future employers that technical knowledge or skill is most effective when it is accompanied by effective communication.

BUSINESS COMMUNICATION AS A CAREER

While communication skills are needed in all careers, there are also a number of career paths for students who wish to make professional communication their primary focus. Many organizations employ communication specialists to manage their internal and external communication functions.

Internal communication takes place within the organization, which for a large company can mean thousands of employees in offices or plants all over the world. Specialists in internal communication are typically responsible for company newsletters and magazines, mass distributions of internal correspondence, policy and procedure manuals, and any other materials exchanged among company personnel. Some professionals in internal communication specialize in visual media and work with in-house presentations and training programs.

Managers of external communication perform many of the same tasks, but their efforts are addressed to audiences outside the company such as customers, potential customers, competitors, regulatory agencies, and the media. Specialists in external communication are frequently responsible for a company's advertising, promotional, and public relations activities. Career options emphasizing similar skills can also be found with companies that provide communication services to other businesses, such as advertising and public relations agencies, direct-mail operations, and producers of multi-media presentations.

To prepare for a career in professional communication you need determination and perhaps some ingenuity. If your school does not offer a major in communication, you may be able to design your own program of courses that serves the same purpose. Find out which departments in your college offer courses in advertising, press relations, public speaking, media arts, and business or technical writing. Keep a portfolio of your communication projects to demonstrate your skills to prospective employers when you are ready to begin your career.

Integration and Transition

As the Recurring Themes model suggests, communication and teamwork undergird all activities in a business. These skills are essential to the success of a business and the success of your business career. This chapter has reminded you to begin now to develop the professional writing and speaking skills that will mark you as an outstanding job candidate. Those skills include the ability to write effective letters, memos, and reports; the ability to use a computer efficiently as a communication tool; and the ability to function productively in a team.

Chapter 3 focuses on Economics, another recurring theme. As you study that chapter, you will learn why you should master the basic principles of economics, what economists do, and the value of a major or a minor in economics.

Discussion and Action

1. Explain the significance of communication and teamwork in business today.
2. What is the primary purpose of all business communication? Give examples to demonstrate your understanding of that purpose.
3. How does business writing differ from other kinds of academic writing?
4. Identify and explain seven guides to improve your writing.
5. In what ways does a business presentation differ from a public address?
6. Identify and give examples of six task-oriented behaviors that you should practice while working with a team.
7. Identify and give examples of five process-oriented behaviors that you should practice while working with a team.
8. Identify and give examples of five dysfunctional behaviors that you should avoid while working with a team.
9. If you have had experience working with a team, either in a class or on the job, describe the experience to your classmates. What functional and dysfunctional behaviors were exhibited in the group? Did the group achieve its goal? Why or why not?

10. Select a topic that is familiar to you but may not be familiar to your class-mates. Prepare, practice, and deliver a three-minute presentation about that topic. Follow the planning, practice, and delivery guides given in this chapter. Examples of appropriate topics are a favorite hobby, an unforget-table person who has influenced your life, a unique travel experience, your career choice, or any other topic approved by your instructor.

11. Search the Internet or your library for a journal or magazine article that emphasizes the importance of communication, teamwork, or computer competence in business. Summarize the article in a one-page memoran-dum to your instructor.

REFERENCES

AXELROD, R., and C. COOPER (1994). *The St. Martin's guide to writing*, 4th ed. New York: St. Martin's Press.

BENNE, K. D., and P. SHEATS (1948). Functional roles of group members. *Journal of Social Issues*, Spring, pp. 41–49.

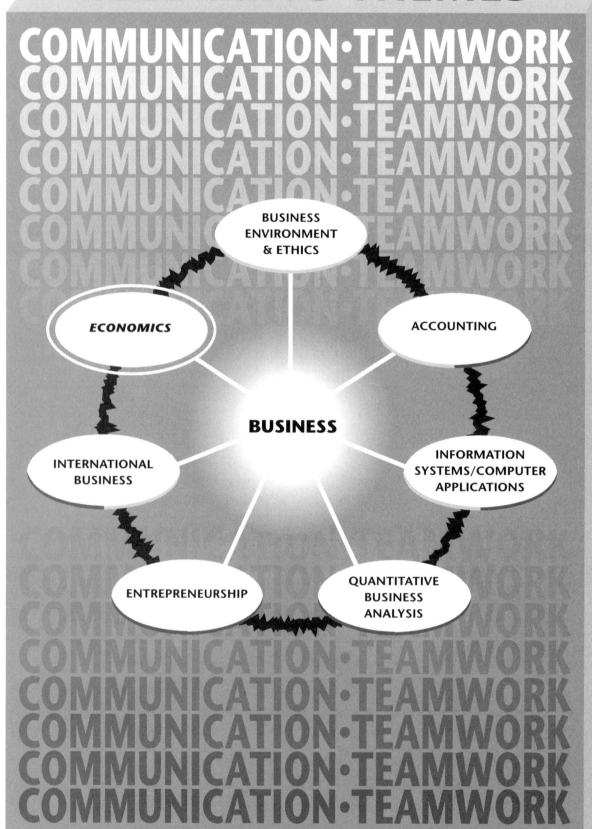

RECURRING THEMES

COMMUNICATION·TEAMWORK

BUSINESS
ENVIRONMENT
& ETHICS

ACCOUNTING

ECONOMICS

BUSINESS

INTERNATIONAL
BUSINESS

INFORMATION
SYSTEMS/COMPUTER
APPLICATIONS

ENTREPRENEURSHIP

QUANTITATIVE
BUSINESS
ANALYSIS

CHAPTER 3

ECONOMICS

OBJECTIVES

After you have read this chapter and completed related activities, you should be able to:

1. Give a general description of the subject of economics.

2. Describe the role of economics in the business curriculum.

3. Describe how a student may eventually use knowledge of economics in her or his career.

4. Describe typical tasks performed by economists in business and government organizations.

5. Begin to evaluate whether you should pursue a major or minor in economics.

Economics appears in the Recurring Themes model, indicating that all areas of business depend on economic information and analytical skills to operate successfully. For that reason, a basic understanding of economics will help you throughout your business curriculum and as you launch your career in business.

In this chapter you will be given a brief history of economics in higher education, an introduction to the subject of economics and its role in the business curriculum, and an overview of careers in economics.

ECONOMICS IN HIGHER EDUCATION

Economics has a long—and sometimes colorful—history in higher education. Thomas Cooper, former president of South Carolina College (now called the University of South Carolina), first began teaching economics in

1825. This was quite possibly the first economics course taught in an American university, although a similar claim is made by Columbia University in New York.

At that time, there were usually about five professors at South Carolina College teaching around 200 students. Each received an annual salary of $2,000 plus on-campus housing and meals at the dining hall. This salary remained unchanged until the beginning of the Civil War. Nonetheless, professors who thought like economists realized that during this period they had received a 10 percent real wage hike, as this was a period of deflation. Moreover, this income was well above that received by the average South Carolinian, leaving professors second only to the state's most prominent lawyers and plantation owners in income. In today's money, those professors earned around $14,000 a year, plus the cost of a dorm room and a meal plan.

A professor's life was not perfect, however. While living on campus, professors were expected to be the equivalent of today's dorm monitors. They had to break up unruly parties, illegal card games, dining hall food fights, and the occasional pistol duel between gentlemen. Francis Lieber succeeded Thomas Cooper as an economics teacher in the mid-1830s. He was known as a strict disciplinarian and therefore a worthy challenge to the more mischievous students. The tradition developed of slipping into Lieber's stable late at night, shaving his horse's tail, and making enough noise to awaken the professor. The middle-aged Lieber would then give chase in his nightclothes, cursing in his native German. The students would flee along a pre-selected route, climbing over the brick wall that surrounded the campus. Professors eventually found excuses for living off campus.

Other notable economists at American universities include Thorstein Veblen, who taught at the University of Chicago from 1892 to 1906. His book, *The Theory of the Leisure Class* (1899), introduced the term *conspicuous consumption*. He proposed that people buy many goods not for personal use, but for the impression their purchases make on others. He cited the example of large picture windows that many wealthy people of the time had on the front of their houses. The windows gave them a clear view of their neighbor's picture window across the street, whereas the back of the house, facing an attractive yard or garden, had only ordinary windows. Veblen himself gave little concern to the impression he made on others. His suits were old and wrinkled, and he washed his dishes in the yard with a garden hose.

The study of economics as it is known today owes much to the Nobel prize-winning economist Paul Samuelson. As a newly-hired assistant professor at M.I.T., he felt that the serious, fine-print textbooks of the day were not the best way to learn. In 1948, he wrote a new principles of economics book, filled with explanatory charts, diagrams, and everyday examples of economic concepts. It has gone through 15 editions, sold 3.5 million copies, and has been translated into 46 languages. A new era in textbooks is beginning, as authors compete to bring out books with Internet sites and software tutorials. The publishing world was recently stunned by the announced $1.4 million advance paid by Dryden Press for *Economics Principles* by Harvard Professor Greg Mankiw. Will the publisher's gamble pay off? At any rate, some economics professors like Mankiw, even after allowing for inflation, now earn more than the $2,000 paid to Thomas Cooper in 1825.

THE SUBJECT OF ECONOMICS

Economics is a study of the impact on society of scarce resources and unlimited desires. This means that every decision about what goods to produce involves a *cost*, or a lost opportunity to produce something else. Similarly, a decision to produce a product in a particular way involves a lost opportunity to produce it in a different manner. In addition, the pursuit by individuals for more material goods means that they react to *incentives*, such as buying more during a sale or selecting college majors that promise higher-paying jobs.

This interaction of costs and incentives is most clearly seen in the operation of markets. Every day, individuals and the business firms and governments they work for buy and sell a dizzying array of goods, services, and resources. Therefore, a key goal of economics is to explain how markets operate, and how the prices determined in markets affect you as a consumer, business owner, or employee.

As a business student, you will be studying how firms are managed with the goal of obtaining profits. Since you will be operating in a market environment, you need to understand markets and the economic forces that drive them. The economics component of your business curriculum is designed to help you see how you and your firm fit into the market processes of capitalism.

Economics is divided into several subject areas. The major classifications are macroeconomics and microeconomics. *Macroeconomics* concentrates on the economy's business cycle. Macroeconomics tries to answer questions like, "What determines the unemployment rate and the inflation rate?" and "What government policies should be undertaken to prevent recessions and maintain the real value of the money used in our economy?"

Microeconomics looks more closely at the behavior of individual consumers, workers, and business firms. Typical microeconomics questions are, "Why do buyers in a market tend to purchase less when prices are higher?" "Why do sellers in a market tend to produce more when prices are higher?" and "Under what circumstances might exceptions to this behavior occur?"

Within these two broad areas, economics is broken down further into specialized topics. Some economists are experts on the monetary sector, while others concentrate on international trade or labor markets. The typical economics professor specializes in two or three topics. When not teaching one of the required general courses, professors will teach upper-level classes in the fields in which they do academic research.

Economics in the Undergraduate Business Curriculum

Most business administration programs require their students to take at least one course in the principles of economics. In some schools macro- and microeconomics may be combined into one course; in others the two areas may be dealt with separately. This survey of economics fundamentals provides a broad picture of the global economy, the national economy, the price system, competition, supply and demand, and an analysis of decisions by consumers and business firms. The course is usually required during the first or second year of the business curriculum because it provides an understanding of the economic system and develops key concepts, which are built upon in other business courses. For example, demand and the analysis of consumer behavior are foundations for marketing courses, and the concepts of capital and investment are developed further in business finance courses.

Economics electives are also an important part of the program of study for many business students. Popular economics electives include courses such as International Economics, Government and Business, Labor Economics, Managerial Economics, Public Finance, Health Economics, and Law and Economics.

The Economics Major

The economics major may be offered in either a school of business or a college of liberal arts. In some universities the major is offered in both colleges. When the major is taken in a business school, the degree earned is usually the Bachelor of Science with a major in Economics; in a liberal arts college, the degree may be a Bachelor of Arts. Under either option, you should be able to design a program that best satisfies your interests.

For example, if you want to combine your economics major with a second major (economics and finance is a popular combination), you would be wise to take four upper-level economics courses beyond Principles of Economics. Those courses might include Intermediate Microeconomics, Intermediate Macroeconomics, and two electives chosen to complement your career goals.

If you would like to attain a deeper background in economics, a more intensive economics major would likely consist of eight courses beyond Principles. These should include Intermediate Microeconomics, Intermediate Macroeconomics, possibly a senior seminar and several electives chosen to complement your career goals. This intensive option is particularly recommended if you are interested in later obtaining a graduate degree in economics.

Economics as Pre-MBA or Pre-Law Degree

The economics major provides an excellent foundation for subsequent study in an MBA program. The business economics concentration, with its emphasis on analytical skills, prepares the student for the more technical emphasis of graduate study in business administration. The economics major also provides an opportunity for students to be grounded in international trade and international monetary economics, an important background for managers in the global economy.

An economics major is also excellent preparation for law school. Although law schools generally do not recommend a specific major, most schools note that pre-law students should choose courses which require significant amounts of reading, writing, analysis, and oral discussion. The advantages of an economics major for law school preparation are its emphasis on the use of logical analysis and its reputation as one of the more rigorous and difficult social sciences to master. If you are motivated to excel, then it is not too early to begin thinking about law school and how coursework in economics can prepare you for that goal.

CAREERS IN ECONOMICS

To help you decide whether you want to pursue a career in economics, this section presents information about what economists do, where they work, the training and personal qualities required to be an economist, and the job outlook and potential earnings for economists.

What Economists Do

Economists study the ways a society distributes scarce resources such as land, labor, raw materials, and machinery to produce goods and services. They conduct research, collect and analyze data, monitor economic trends, and develop forecasts. They might research topics such as energy costs, inflation, interest rates, farm prices, rents, imports, or employment levels.

Most economists are concerned with practical applications of economic policy in a particular area. They use their understanding of economic relationships to advise businesses and other organizations, including insurance companies, banks, securities firms, industry and trade associations, labor unions, and government agencies. Economists use mathematical models to develop programs predicting the nature and length of business cycles, the effects of inflation on the economy, or the effects of tax legislation on unemployment levels.

Economists devise methods and procedures for obtaining the data they need. For example, sampling techniques may be used to conduct a survey, and various mathematical modeling techniques may be used to develop forecasts. Being able to present economic and statistical concepts in a meaningful way is particularly important for an economist whose research is directed toward making policy for an organization. The economist must review and analyze relevant data, prepare applicable tables and charts, and report the results in clear, concise language that can be understood by noneconomists.

Economists who work for government agencies may assess economic conditions in the United States or abroad in an attempt to estimate the economic effects of specific changes in legislation or public policy. For example, they may study areas such as how the dollar's fluctuation against foreign currencies affects import and export levels. The majority of government economists work in the areas of agriculture, labor, or quantitative analysis; but almost every area of government employs economists. For example, economists in the U.S. Department of Commerce study domestic production, distribution, and consumption of commodities or services, while economists employed with the Bureau of Labor Statistics analyze data on prices, wages, employment, productivity, and safety and health. An economist working in state or local government might analyze data on trade and commerce, industrial growth, and employment and unemployment rates in order to project employment trends.

Where Economists Work

Economists and marketing research analysts held about 48,000 jobs in 1994. Approximately 80 percent of those analysts were employed in private industry—in particular, economic and marketing research firms, management consulting firms, banks, securities and commodities brokers, and computer and data processing companies. The remainder, primarily economists, were employed by a wide range of government agencies, mostly in state government. The Departments of Labor, Agriculture, and Commerce are the largest federal employers of economists. A number of economists combine a full-time job in government or business with part-time or consulting work in academia or another setting.

Employment of economists is concentrated in large cities. Some economists work abroad for companies with major international operations, for U.S. Government agencies, and for international organizations like the World Bank and the United Nations. Besides the jobs described here, many economists hold faculty positions in colleges and universities.

Training and Personal Qualities Required of Economists

In the private sector, persons who hold a bachelor's degree in economics often work in areas in which economics complements other skills they have. A limited number of federal government positions are available to economists who hold a bachelor's degree. The best career options for business economists in the corporate world often require some graduate training.

Undergraduate Education

Persons who graduate with a bachelor's degree in economics through the year 2005 will face keen competition for the limited number of economist positions for which they qualify. However, they will qualify for a number of other positions in which they can take advantage of their economic knowledge by conducting research, developing surveys, or analyzing data. Many graduates with bachelor's degrees will find entry-level jobs in industry and business as management or sales trainees or administrative assistants. Economists with good quantitative skills are qualified for research assistant positions in a broad range of fields.

Economists are concerned with understanding and interpreting financial matters, among other subjects. Jobs in this area include financial managers, financial analysts, underwriters, actuaries, securities and financial services sales workers, credit analysts, loan officers, and budget officers. In addition, economists who meet state certification requirements may become high school economics teachers. The demand for secondary school economics teachers is expected to grow as economics becomes an increasingly important and popular course.

In the federal government, candidates for entry-level economist positions must have a bachelor's degree with a minimum of 21 semester hours of economics and 3 hours of statistics, accounting, or calculus. Competition is keen for positions that require only a bachelor's degree; work experience or superior academic performance is likely to be influential. Additional training will be required for advancement.

Graduate Education

Candidates who hold a master's degree in economics have much better employment prospects than bachelor's degree holders. Many businesses, research and consulting firms, and government agencies seek master's degree holders who have strong computer and quantitative skills and can perform complex research, but do not command the higher salary of a person who holds a doctor's degree.

Graduate training is required for most private-sector economist jobs and for advancement to more responsible positions. Economics curricula include many specialties at the graduate level, such as advanced economic theory, econometrics, international economics, and labor economics. Students should select graduate schools strong in specialties in which they are interested. Some schools help graduate students find internships or part-time employment in government agencies, economic consulting firms, or financial institutions.

If you enjoy teaching, you may turn your interests in that direction. For a job as an instructor in many junior or community colleges, a master's degree is the minimum requirement. In most colleges and universities, however, a Ph.D. is necessary for appointment as an instructor. A Ph.D. and extensive publications in academic journals are required for long-term employment in a university professorship.

Whether working in government, industry, research organizations, or consulting firms, economists who have a graduate degree usually qualify for more responsible research and administrative positions. A Ph.D. is necessary for top economist positions in many organizations. Moreover, many corporation and government executives have a strong background in economics.

Personal Qualities

Persons considering careers as economists should be able to work accurately because much time is spent on data analysis. Patience and persistence are necessary qualities because economists must spend long hours on independent study and problem solving. At the same time, they must be able to work well with others. Economists must be able to present their findings in a clear and meaningful way, both orally and in writing.

A strong background in economic theory, mathematics, statistics, and econometrics provides the basis for acquiring any specialty within the field. Individuals skilled in quantitative techniques and their application to economic modeling and forecasting, including the use of computers, coupled with good communications skills, should have the best job opportunities.

Job and Salary Outlook

Employment of economists and marketing research analysts is expected to grow faster than the average for all occupations through the year 2005. Most job openings, however, are likely to result from the need to replace experienced workers who transfer to other occupations, retire, or leave the labor force for other reasons.

Opportunities for economists should be best in private industry, especially in research, testing, and consulting firms that do economic research for businesses. Contemporary business trends should spur demand for economists. Those trends include the growing complexity of the global economy and increased reliance on quantitative methods for analyzing business trends, forecasting sales, and planning purchasing and production. The continued need for economic analysis in virtually every industry should result in additional jobs for economists. Employment of economists in the federal government should decline in line with the rate of growth projected for the federal workforce as a whole. Slower-than-average employment growth is expected among economists in state and local government.

According to a 1995 salary survey by the National Association of Colleges and Employers, persons with a bachelor's degree in economics received offers averaging $27,600 a year. The median base salary of business economists in 1994 was $70,000, according to a survey by the National Association of Business Economists. Ninety-two percent of the respondents held advanced degrees. The highest salaries were reported by those who had a Ph.D., with a median salary of $80,000. Master's degree holders earned a median salary of $62,000, while bachelor's degree holders earned $60,500. The highest paid business economists were in the securities and investment industry, which reported a median income of $95,000, followed by the nondurable manufacturing industry at $94,000 and the banking industry at $85,000. The lowest paid were in academia, wholesale and retail trade, and publishing.

The Federal Government recognizes education and experience in certifying applicants for entry-level positions. In general, the entry salary for economists having a bachelor's degree averaged about $18,700 a year in 1995; however, those with superior academic records could begin at $23,200. Those having a master's degree could qualify for positions at an annual salary of $28,300. Those with a Ph.D. could begin at $34,300, while some individuals with experience and an advanced degree could start at $41,100. Starting salaries were slightly more in selected areas where the prevailing local pay was higher. Economists in the federal government in nonsupervisory, supervisory, and managerial positions averaged around $59,030 a year in 1995.

INTEGRATION AND TRANSITION

Economics is the study of how society uses resources to satisfy unlimited wants. An economics major may lead to careers in research and management in the financial, manufacturing, services, and government sectors of the economy. An economics major is also a valuable foundation for graduate study in business or law. All business persons must understand the fundamentals of the economic system in which business operates; therefore, an economics minor is a natural complement to business majors, such as accounting, finance, management, operations management, or marketing.

As the Recurring Themes model indicates, communication and economics are two themes that pervade all courses in business and all business operations. Another recurring theme is how the business environment, the company's stakeholders, and a sense of corporate social responsibility influence business activities. That theme is discussed in Chapter 4.

DISCUSSION AND ACTION

1. Define the following terms:
   - economics
   - microeconomics
   - macroeconomics
   - conspicuous consumption

2. What areas within economics interest you the most? Why? How might you turn that interest into a career opportunity?

3. What are some of the advantages of taking an economics major in your undergraduate curriculum? What are the disadvantages?

4. What are the advantages of taking economics electives or an economics minor to complement another business major?

5. Identify and interview an economics professor in your college. Report the results of the interview in a 3-minute presentation to your class. The following questions may guide your interview:
   - When did you first become interested in economics? Why did you become interested?
   - What kinds of consulting or work experiences have you had? How did you apply your knowledge of economics in those experiences?
   - What undergraduate or graduate courses do you teach? What is the major focus of each course? Who should take the course?
   - What advice would you give to a student who is considering a career in economics?
   - What advice would you give to a student who enjoys studying economics but does not want to be an economist?

6. Identify and interview an economist who works for a local business, such as a bank, an insurance company, a securities firm, or a research agency. Ask the person to describe a typical working day. Write a brief summary (one or two pages) of your findings.

7. If you studied economics in high school, share your experiences with your classmates. What was the primary focus of the course? What were your favorite topics or projects in the course? In what ways has the course helped you in your daily living? In what ways has the course helped you to understand economics issues at the local, state, or national level?

8. Review your local newspaper. Find one story or editorial that discusses the impact of economic forces on individuals or a business. Bring the story to class to share with your classmates.

9. Visit the Career Center on your campus. Find additional information about job opportunities for a person with an economics major. Be prepared to give a brief oral presentation (2–3 minutes) of your findings. Be selective as you prepare for the presentation. Follow the guides for presentations given in Chapter 2.

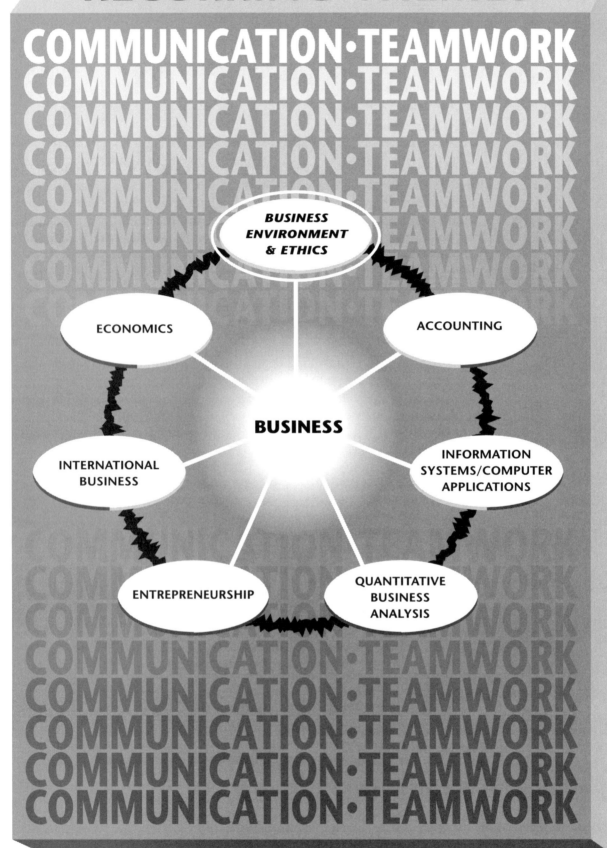

CHAPTER 4

THE BUSINESS ENVIRONMENT

OBJECTIVES

After you have read this chapter and completed related activities, you should be able to:

1. Identify elements of the remote environment and describe how they may affect a business.

2. Identify elements of the direct-action environment and describe how they may affect a business.

3. Identify internal stakeholders of a business and describe how they may affect a business.

4. Identify levels of corporate social responsibility and describe specific actions that a company might engage in at each level.

The presence of Business Environment and Ethics in the Recurring Themes model suggests that this theme will arise in many of your courses. Moreover, it suggests that effective business managers and executives are continually aware of the forces in the business environment and how they may affect the business.

In this chapter, the key elements of a business firm's environment and their potential impact on the management of the firm will be discussed. Then the needs of the internal stakeholders of the firm—employees/managers, owners/stockholders, and members of the board of directors—will be analyzed. Finally, the chapter will introduce how the top management of a firm might go about resolving the claims of various stakeholders, including the concept of corporate social responsibility.

TODAY'S COMPLEX BUSINESS ENVIRONMENT

The business environment has become extremely turbulent and complex for United States firms in recent years. For example, the rate of technological change and the extent of foreign competition have increased substantially in many industries. In the late 1960s Japanese automobiles were considered to be cheap jokes. Today Japanese firms successfully challenge automobile makers all over the world.

Additional pressures have come from groups outside the firm, such as customers, suppliers, consumer groups, environmentalists, government agencies, and local communities, who demand that the firm's managers meet their needs. Thus, as managers make business decisions, they must consider the desires of many groups in addition to customers and stockholders.

REMOTE ENVIRONMENT

The remote environment of the firm consists of broad societal forces that may affect the firm in two ways:

1. The forces may influence the external stakeholders of the firm, who in turn will make demands on the firm.
2. The forces may create the need or opportunity for new stakeholder groups to come into existence.

The five key forces in the remote or external environment are economic variables, technological variables, sociocultural variables, political variables, and the international arena.

Economic Variables

Such variables as the costs of labor and raw materials have a direct impact on the firm by affecting the cost of production. For example, in the garment industry the cost of labor has influenced many American firms to assemble their products in underdeveloped countries, such as the Dominican Republic, where labor costs are a fraction of what they are in the continental United States.

The state of the economy often affects different firms, even those in the same industry, in different ways. For example, when the economy is in a recession, the sales of new cars fall while the sales for firms servicing and replacing parts for old cars rise.

Technological Variables

New technology can give firms a competitive advantage or cause them to go bankrupt, depending on their foresight and ability to develop and market the results of new technology. For example, in the late 1960s key actors in the Swiss watch industry thought the new quartz movement technology which they possessed would never replace skilled watchmakers. Thus, the rights to use the new technology were sold to a virtually unknown Japanese firm, Seiko. Today Seiko is the world's leading watchmaker, and employment in the Swiss watch industry has declined by approximately 90 percent.

Sociocultural Variables

Sociocultural factors can be broken down into three major categories: population demographics, lifestyle variables, and social values.

Three major factors influence demographics in the United States today. First, life expectancy is increasing. It is expected that the percentage of the population over age 65 will increase from approximately 12 percent in 1990 to around 18 percent in 2030. Second, the "baby boomers," individuals born between 1946 and 1970, are reaching middle age. Third, the Hispanic and black segments of the population are growing more rapidly than the remainder of the population. It is difficult to state exactly how these factors will affect individual firms and society as a whole. One can surmise, however, that the aging of the population will place increasing pressure on the social infrastructure and provide opportunities in healthcare and related industries. The growth of non-Caucasian populations and the increasing number of women in the workforce raise the importance of recognizing, honoring, and managing cultural diversity. These issues must be positively addressed by the top management of business firms, not-for-profit organizations, and government agencies.

Lifestyle changes can either threaten established firms or provide new opportunities. New firms and established firms that keep up-to-date with emerging trends soon recognize opportunities to satisfy unmet customer needs. For example, the "traditional" American family with a father who works, two or more children, and a mother who is not in the workforce now constitutes less than 10 percent of family units. Another trend is a concern about healthy diet and exercise. These two trends pose a threat to products such as fast food with a high fat content, while presenting opportunities to companies that provide products and services for dual-career and single-parent families and for diet- and exercise-conscious individuals.

Societal values are particularly important as they come to play in the workplace. Some managers and workers think participative management is imperative today, while others lament the perceived decline in the work ethic among today's workers. According to Stoner and Freeman (1992, p. 72), in recent years changes in social values have reduced the U.S. society's commitment to hiring quotas and industry regulation and have increased its concern about the costs and benefits of new technology, particularly in healthcare and pollution abatement.

What these sociocultural changes mean is that managers must keep abreast of social trends, particularly those that are related to their customers and their labor markets. A company's success or failure depends on its sensitivity to these factors.

Political Variables

Generally the political climate in the United States has been favorable to business. However, it has varied from the very friendly climate during the boom years of the 1920s to the deep distrust of the 1960s. That distrust resulted in the passage of major legislation involving the employment rights of "disadvantaged" groups such as minorities and women, pension rights, workplace safety, product safety, and pollution abatement.

In recent years the number of interest groups that try to influence businesses' actions have increased substantially, and the media have occasionally exhibited a considerable anti-business bias. These conditions place increasing pressure on the top management of firms to see that policies and procedures to ensure ethical behavior are in place and that the public relations function operates effectively. In fact, in many large firms today the CEO (Chief Executive Officer) spends the majority of her or his time dealing with external constituencies rather than dealing with the internal affairs of the firm.

The International Arena

Thirty years ago the United States was a largely isolated economy with less than 10 percent of its commerce involved in international trade. Today about 20 percent of the U.S. GDP (Gross Domestic Product) is connected to international trade, and whole industries, such as electronics, are dominated by foreign firms. Chapter 11 of this text discusses the increasingly important international business arena.

DIRECT-ACTION ENVIRONMENT/EXTERNAL STAKEHOLDERS

Some external groups have a direct impact on the firm and can significantly affect the nature and complexity of its environment; thus, these groups are referred to as the *direct-action environment*. Since these groups have a direct interest in the performance of the firm, they are also referred to as *external stakeholders*. The principal external stakeholders of most firms are competitors, customers, suppliers, government agencies, financial institutions, local communities, and special-interest groups.

Competitors

Competitors have a direct and significant impact on the firm. A firm's managers must seek to gain competitive advantages for the firm, to be better than its competition, and to minimize the threat that results from competitors' strategic competitive moves. Moreover, competitors expect the firm to abide by societal and industry norms with regard to the rules of the game.

Customers

Customers are critical to the survival of the firm. Managers must design strategies which result in the production of goods and services that appeal to customers. According to Professor Michael Porter of the Harvard Business

School, firms may be successful if the market sees them as the low cost/high quality producer; if they pursue a differentiation strategy by producing a superior product; or if they use a focus strategy, like Mercedes Benz, and appeal only to a segment of the market (Porter, 1980). What management wants to avoid is trying to be everything to everybody, and end up not being distinctive.

Suppliers

Securing adequate sources of supplies is critical to the success of the firm. For example, for several years Sears secured an advantage over its competitors in sales of appliances by dominating its suppliers, like Whirlpool, and buying from them at low prices. This practice allowed Sears to deliver superior value to its customers, while making an above-average profit.

Government Agencies

Government agencies implement legislation and place considerable restraints on managerial actions. The impact of government on business is evidenced by the following facts (Steiner and Steiner, 1994, pp. 260–261).

1. Government purchases over 15 percent of the goods produced in the United States.
2. Government prescribes the rules of the game.
3. Government promotes and subsidizes business.
4. Government regulates areas in which the market has been seen to fail or where it is perceived that reliance on a free market would not be efficient.

Some of the areas in which government regulations impinge on business are taxation, pollution control, occupational safety, product safety, consumer protection, and equal employment laws. The extent of government involvement in business affairs has increased substantially over the last 35 years.

Financial Institutions

Financial institutions handle day-to-day transactions by business firms, supply funds through loans and other financial devices, provide insurance, and manage employee pension funds. Financial institutions frequently influence managerial decisions by applying conditions to loans and placing pressure on the management of the firm when the firm is not performing well.

Local Communities

Local communities, particularly where the firm is a major player, want the firm to provide stable employment, support community activities, and not adversely affect the health and environment of the community. The quality and values of the labor force of the community have a critical impact on the profitability of the firm. It is not surprising that most Japanese automobile plants in the United States have been located in small communities with a strong work ethic and an absence of the adversarial union-management relationship that hampered much of the U.S. automobile industry for a long time.

Other Groups

In recent years the number and presence of special-interest groups in this country have grown rapidly.

Consumer and environmental groups have affected the policies of many companies. For example, concern over the Northern Spotted Owl has shut down much of the timber industry in the Pacific Northwest.

Consumer and environmental groups receive media publicity, much of which is adverse to firms. These groups sometimes use annual corporate stockholder meetings to publicly vent their dissatisfaction with management practices.

INTERNAL STAKEHOLDERS

Internal stakeholders are also critical to the success of the firm. The key internal stakeholders are employees and managers, owners or stockholders, and the board of directors.

Employees/Managers

If a firm is to succeed, its managers must develop a favorable work environment with regard to wages, fringe benefits, and working conditions. Increasingly, employees wish to be empowered; that is, they want to have a major say in decisions affecting their work. Many managers wonder how to maintain employee loyalty in an environment in which company downsizing is common. Another threat to employee loyalty is the reality that over 25 percent of the workforce is employed on a temporary or part-time basis.

Managerial employees are also critical to firm survival. A major challenge lies in designing compensation systems and incentives to motivate managers to perform in a way that ensures above-average returns for stockholders

Owners/Stockholders

In most small firms, which constitute over 98 percent of all business establishments in the United States, the top management and the owners are one and the same. In large firms, however, about 60 percent of all stock is owned by large institutions, such as mutual funds. These stakeholders expect the firm to earn above-average returns and to be perceived as being socially responsible; that is, not to incur unfavorable publicity. Dissatisfaction on the part of stockholders can lead to declining stock prices, difficulty in obtaining additional funds, replacement of the top management of the firm, or the acquisition of the firm by another firm.

Board of Directors

The board of directors is responsible for overseeing the firm's management. Traditionally, boards took little action unless firm performance was inadequate. Today directors are supposed to monitor firm performance closely and monitor the overall direction of corporate strategy. There is increasing pressure to diversify board membership by including women, minorities, and representatives of key stakeholder groups on boards. Furthermore, there is pressure to have greater numbers of board members who are not actively involved in the management of the firm. Lawsuits against board members for not adequately performing their duties have risen rapidly over the last two decades; consequently, boards have become much more active in the oversight of the firm.

STAKEHOLDER MANAGEMENT AND CORPORATE SOCIAL RESPONSIBILITY

Traditionally economic theory held that a manager's sole responsibility was to maximize returns to stockholders. Today managers must also recognize the claims of other legitimate stakeholders. Pearce and Robinson (1997, pp. 46–47) suggest a four-step process for incorporating stakeholder claims into the firm's strategy-making process:

1. *Identifying stakeholders.* This is critical. Key stakeholders will vary by industry, location, technology employed, and several other variables.

2. *Understanding the nature of claims.* This is a difficult step because the perspectives and values of many stakeholders differ from those of the firm's managers. Although it is sometimes difficult to understand and communicate with critics, managers must attempt to understand the demands of the stakeholders.

3. *Reconciling claims and setting priorities.* Conflict is often present at this step. For example, many claims of governmental agencies and the general public consume funds and hurt profitability, which runs contrary to the primary claim of stockholders. Therefore, management must set priorities and make trade-offs.

4. *Coordinating the claims with company strategy.* Stakeholder claims are only one element affecting the selection of company strategy. Other factors include market opportunities, company capabilities, and corporate philosophy.

Beginning in the early 1900s, the CEOs of several large companies began to argue that the role of top management was to be a trustee of society's interests, to balance interests between the firm's main constituents, and to provide a service to society (Steiner and Steiner, 1994, p. 109). These ideas were the forerunner to the concept of corporate social responsibility.

There are many definitions of corporate social responsibility, depending on one's point of view. A moderate one that has been used widely was provided by Professor Keith Davis, who taught at Arizona State University for many years. He stated:

> ...it [social responsibility] refers to the firm's consideration of a response to issues beyond the narrow economic, technical, and legal requirements of the firm. It is the firm's obligation to evaluate in its decision-making process the effects of its decisions on the external social system in a manner that will accomplish social benefits along with the traditional economic gains which the firm seeks. It means that social responsibility begins where the law ends (Davis, 1973, pp. 35–36).

This statement clearly supports the basic tenets of stakeholder management. However, it does not indicate priorities. Professor Archie Carroll of the University of Georgia has identified priorities in his pyramid of social responsibilities (Carroll, 1979, 1991). He holds that there are four types of social responsibilities. Starting at the bottom of the pyramid, those responsibilities are economic, legal, ethical, and philanthropic (Figure 4-1).

1. *Economic responsibilities.* These involve economic performance. Clearly, a firm cannot survive unless it satisfies the needs of customers, employees, and stockholders/owners.
2. *Legal responsibilities.* These encompass obeying the law. The legal responsibility does not preclude lobbying and taking positions regarding the validity of public policy. In fact, the top managers of large firms are much more involved in public affairs today than they were 30 years ago.

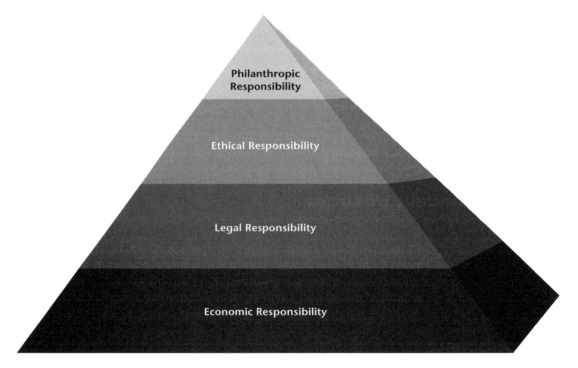

Figure 4-1 *Pyramid of corporate social responsibility.*

3. *Ethical responsibilities.* These involve meeting public expectations that have not been codified into law. Since many issues at this level fall into gray areas, company views may differ from public views. This is why the top management of most large firms pays a great deal of attention to ethical issues. Carroll argues that it is critical for a firm to deal with and resolve social problems that it causes, such as pollution.

4. *Philanthropic responsibilities.* This involves activities such as making philanthropic donations or providing day-care centers for employees' children. Carroll contends that philanthropy is the company's least important responsibility and that the extent to which it is pursued is a matter of company philosophy.

Because of perceived ethical problems related to business practices, the top management of companies, particularly of large firms, pays a great deal of attention to the gray areas. Over 90 percent of the Fortune 500 firms have written codes for ethical conduct. The codes deal with what to do and not to do in given situations. Ethical training programs are common. Many boards of directors also have ethical audit committees.

According to Carroll (1987), the problem is not that managers are unethical, but rather that they have not been trained to be aware of the ethical implications of everyday business decisions. It appears that the managers of many companies are expending considerable effort to deal with these problems.

SUMMARY AND IMPLICATIONS FOR BUSINESS ADMINISTRATION STUDENTS

While making strategic decisions, the top management of business firms, particularly large firms, must consider a myriad of stakeholders. The public expects a firm not only to produce quality products and services at a favorable price but also to be a good citizen and deal with the claims of numerous stakeholders of the firm.

Analyzing and responding to these claims requires support and action by top management and the assistance of numerous staff specialists. Among the types of specialists needed are economic and social forecasters; public affairs and public relations specialists; community relations and community affairs specialists; and human resource specialists. The kinds of career preparation discussed in the chapters on communication, economics, and management may lead to positions directly related to maintaining favorable relationships with a company's many stakeholders. Although these positions are rarely entry-level positions and many of them require advanced degrees, business administration graduates might advance to these positions later in their careers. However, first-line managers (supervisors) and entry-level employees also need to be aware of the social and economic issues affecting business and need to be skilled in dealing with stakeholders.

INTEGRATION AND TRANSITION

You have examined three parts of the Recurring Themes model: the underlying significance of communication and teamwork in an organization, the economic foundation for all business operations in a market economy, and the need for management to be sensitive to changes in the remote environment as well as the expectations of the firm's external and internal stakeholders. Chapter 5 focuses on another element of the model, the importance of accounting to the successful management of any business or not-for-profit organization.

DISCUSSION AND ACTION

1. Identify five key forces in the external environment that affect businesses. Give an example of each and explain why or how they have an impact on businesses.

2. Identify three types of internal stakeholders. Give an example of how each can affect the operations of a business.

3. What is your concept of corporate social responsibility?

4. Imagine that you are the CEO of a large company with manufacturing plants in Michigan, Ohio, and Indiana. You are considering relocating a manufacturing plant to South Carolina or Mississippi. Using your knowledge from the chapter, what should you consider before you make this decision? Why?

5. Browse the World Wide Web to find the code of ethics for a major U.S. company. Analyze the code by answering these questions:

   • Does the code recognize a responsibility to direct stakeholders? What stakeholders are identified? What is said about that responsibility?

   • Does the code recognize a responsibility to indirect stakeholders? What stakeholders are identified? What is said about that responsibility?

   • What levels of the pyramid of social responsibility are addressed in the code?

   • Based on your analysis of the code, do you think you would want to work for this company? Why?

   As directed by your instructor, present your findings in a written report or an oral presentation to your class.

6. Review your local newspaper or a business magazine. Find a story about a contemporary event or issue that demonstrates a concept presented in this chapter; for example, the impact of the remote environment or external stakeholders on a firm, the concerns of internal stakeholders, or an example of corporate social responsibility. Bring the story to class for analysis and discussion.

REFERENCES

CARROLL, A. B. (1979). A three-dimensional conceptual model of corporate social performance. *Academy of Management Journal*, 4, pp. 497–506.

CARROLL, A. B. (1987). In search of the moral manager. *Business Horizons*, 30(2), pp. 7–15.

CARROLL, A. B. (1991). The pyramid of corporate social responsibility: Toward the moral management of organizational stakeholders. *Business Horizons*, 34(4), pp. 39–48.

DAVIS, K. (1973). The case for and against business assumption of social responsibilities. *Academy of Management Journal*, June, pp. 35–36. In A. B. Carroll, Ed., (1977). *Managing Corporate Social Responsibility*. Boston: Little, Brown, pp. 35–45.

PEARCE, J. A., II and R. B. ROBINSON JR. (1997). *Strategic Management*, 6th ed. Chicago: Irwin.

PORTER, M. E. (1980). *Competitive Strategy*. New York: Free Press.

STEINER, G. A., and J. F. STEINER (1994). *Business, Government, and Society*, 7th ed. New York: McGraw-Hill.

STONER, J. A. F., and R. E. FREEMAN, (1992). *Management* 5th ed. Upper Saddle River, New Jersey: Prentice Hall.

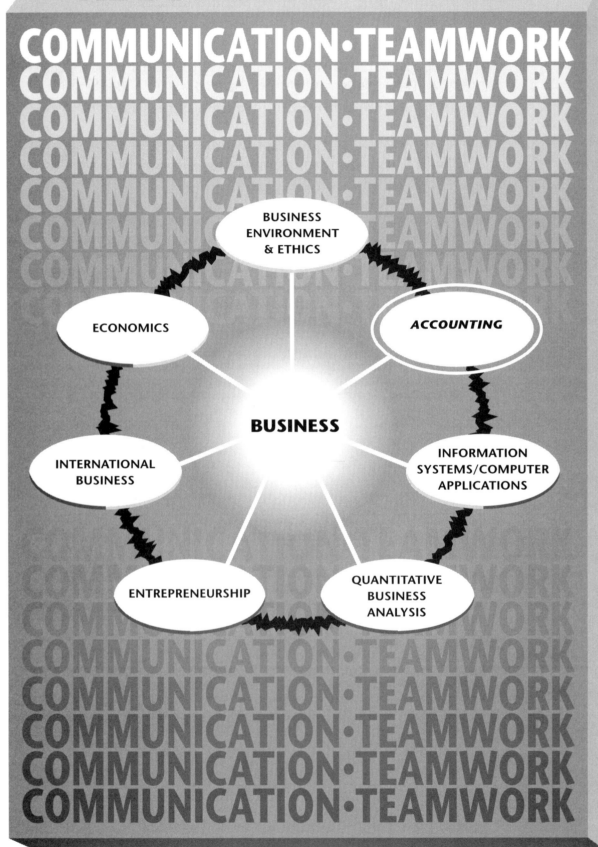

CHAPTER 5

ACCOUNTING

OBJECTIVES

After you have read this chapter and completed related activities, you should be able to:

1. Identify the general skills needed to become a successful accountant or CPA (Certified Public Accountant).

2. Identify requirements for professional certification as a CPA, CMA (Certified Management Accountant), or CIA (Certified Internal Auditor).

3. Identify job opportunities and typical career paths for accountants.

The accounting profession is one of the fastest growing professions in the world. The tremendous growth of the global marketplace and information technologies has greatly increased demand for competent and ethical professionals who are fluent in the language of business. The role of an accountant ranks among the most demanding in the American economic community.

As the Recurring Themes model illustrates, the accountant's ability to provide the information necessary to determine and evaluate the past, present, and future economic activities of organizations is vital in the business environment. However, accountants are not simply number crunchers. Whether as an auditor, tax advisor, educator, management consultant, business leader, or government official, an accountant carries out assignments with independence, integrity, and objectivity. Accountants are trained to seek logical solutions to diverse problems while applying sound, ethical judgments.

In this chapter you will be introduced to the general skills required to be an accountant, the more specific requirements for professional certification, and typical career opportunities for accountants.

WHAT SKILLS ARE NEEDED TO BECOME A SUCCESSFUL ACCOUNTANT?

Becoming a successful accountant begins while you are still in college. You need to demonstrate superior scholastic achievement, possess a good technical accounting background, and complement that accounting knowledge with the broad business knowledge obtained from your core business courses and electives. A good foundation in the humanities and other liberal arts subjects is also essential.

You will need other skills to complement your academic preparation. Problem-solving skills are vital. You should be able to analyze, compare, and interpret facts and figures. You have to be a creative thinker because every day you will face issues that need innovative solutions. The answers you come up with are often the difference between being a good accountant or CPA and a great one. In addition, you need to understand business systems and computers. You must know about networks and be familiar with spreadsheets and accounting software.

Good people skills and high ethical standards are also essential. Accounting is a service activity, and you will have to work well with clients and coworkers, both in groups and in one-on-one situations. Therefore communicating well, both verbally and in writing, is essential. Finally, as an accountant, you must have high ethical standards because people rely on the information you provide.

TYPICAL COLLEGE PROGRAMS IN ACCOUNTING

Many colleges offer a four-year undergraduate degree and graduate degrees in accounting. An undergraduate major in accounting generally requires 24 hours of accounting courses in addition to the core business requirements. In some programs, graduate students have the option of specializing in a tax program or a more traditional program. Students who do not have an undergraduate degree in accounting may be required to complete certain prerequisite business and accounting classes before being allowed to enroll in either a Master of Taxation or a Master of Accountancy program. If you are interested in an accounting career, check the degree requirements at your college early in your college career, so that you will be able to complete all requirements in a timely manner.

CERTIFICATION OF ACCOUNTANTS

The three most highly recognized certification programs for accountants are the CPA (Certified Public Accountant), CMA (Certified Management Accountant), and CIA (Certified Internal Auditor). Certification is important to professional accountants because it provides:

- Participation in a recognized professional association
- Opportunities for continuing professional education
- Recognition from peers for obtaining the professional designation
- Additional credentials for the employment market or career ladder

Requirements to Become a CPA

The requirements to become a CPA are governed by state laws. Many states have minimum credit hour requirements for accounting and other business courses. All states require a bachelor's degree or its equivalent. In addition many states have implemented a 150-hour or master's degree requirement. In addition to completion of the required credit hours, all states require successful completion of the CPA exam. Many states also have work experience requirements.

Requirements to Become a CMA

The general requirements for CMA certification are a bachelor's degree or its equivalent, successful completion of the CMA exam, and two years' work experience in managerial or public accounting.

Requirements to Become a CIA

To become a CIA, you must have a bachelor's degree or its equivalent, successfully complete the CIA exam, and have two years' internal auditing experience.

WHAT ARE THE JOB OPPORTUNITIES FOR ACCOUNTANTS?

As the economy strengthens, hiring of accounting staff by accounting firms, businesses, and other employers continues to gain momentum. In 1994, the U.S. Department of Labor's Bureau of Labor Statistics (BLS) predicted that accounting will be one of the 10 fastest-growing industries during the next 10 years. Results of a BLS survey of accounting firms, companies, government agencies, and other employers indicate that there are about 850,000 accountants and auditors in the United States today. U.S. Census data, which is based on how individuals identify their occupations, places the number of accountants and auditors at 1.5 million. The consensus is that the number of accountants and auditors falls somewhere between these two extremes.

With the outlook for hiring better than it has been in many years, there will likely be shortages in certain job categories. In particular, professionals with one to five years of experience are difficult to find. As a result employers are raising the starting salaries for this group faster than they are for others. Companies and firms are also taking a strategic and more flexible approach to hiring, which has strengthened operations substantially. Many employers are having success hiring senior staff from the ranks of middle managers who were made available through downsizing at other companies and firms. Because of their experience, the former managers work with less supervision and greater efficiency. Despite the projected need for accountants and CPAs, competition for new jobs will be fierce. Firms and companies are staffing more efficiently today and asking employees to handle a wider variety of tasks.

Among the emerging specialties are tax accounting, environmental accounting, forensic accounting, software development, entertainment, and telecommunications. Tax specialists will continue to be in high demand as tax codes become more and more complicated. Additionally, professionals skilled in international tax issues should see a dramatic increase in their value. Environmental consultants are needed to help companies avoid penalties for compliance infractions. Forensic accountants are valued for their skills in examining accounting records for fraud or other criminal activity. However, the demand for these specialties varies by region.

Within public accounting, competition has forced firms to place increased emphasis on new business development. As little as five years ago, this function was reserved for partners and senior managers, but today it has become essential for managers at all levels.

The largest accounting firms are meeting the demands of increased competition by expanding their traditional areas of specialization to become full-service providers. Emphasis is being placed on consultancy services, including process improvement and re-engineering; tax accounting, especially sales and international tax; estate planning; and financial planning for individuals and corporations. This emphasis on consulting services has resulted in a new career path for professionals in these firms—the consultant track. Candidates who can assist clients in everything from auditing and tax work to process improvement are highly valued.

Opportunities in small and mid-size public accounting firms are also expanding as those firms take advantage of the growing number of businesses going public. In particular, the auditing function has become very competitive as companies continue shopping actively for low-cost auditing services.

A career in accounting provides individuals with a competitive entry-level salary and long-term growth potential, particularly those who have earned CPA certification. According to the College Placement Council's September 1995 Salary Survey, entry-level salaries for new graduates with bachelor's degrees in accounting averaged about $28,000 during 1994. Entry-level salaries for new graduates with master's degrees averaged about $31,500.

WHAT ARE THE DIFFERENT CAREER PATHS IN ACCOUNTING?

As an accountant, you will have a broad choice of career paths. Opportunities exist in public practice, industry, government, and not-for-profit organizations.

Public Practice

A variety of specialty career paths exist within public practice.

Auditing

Auditing is one of the most important and best-known services provided by CPAs in public practice. To protect consumers and investors, the Securities and Exchange Commission (SEC) requires every publicly-held company to issue an annual financial statement. This financial statement is examined by an independent CPA, and the results are called an *audit*. The CPA's role as an auditor is to examine a company's financial statements in order to assure stockholders and other financial statement users that a company's financial position is reported fairly.

Although privately-held companies are not required to have annual audits, many do so anyway. Privately-held companies that do not undergo an annual audit often engage CPAs to conduct a *review* or *compilation* instead. Both involve an examination of a company's financial statements, although a review contains less assurance than an audit while a compilation contains no assurance.

Environmental Accounting

This is one of the hot growth areas in public accounting. As businesses take a greater interest in environmental issues, CPAs have been getting involved in everything from environmental compliance audits or systems and procedures audits, to handling claims and disputes. Utilities, manufacturers, and chemical companies are particularly affected by environmental issues. As a result, companies in these fields have increasingly turned to CPAs to set up a preventive system to ensure compliance and avoid future claims or disputes, or to provide assistance once legal implications have arisen.

Forensic Accounting

This is another hot growth area for CPAs. The forensic accountant looks beyond the face value of accounting records to determine if fraud has been committed. Also known as an *investigative accountant* or *fraud auditor*, the forensic accountant searches for evidence of criminal conduct or assists in the determination of, or rebuttal of, claimed damages. Investigative accountants are also called in to advise companies on whether to declare bankruptcy or take the necessary steps to remain solvent. In addition to investigative accounting, the forensic accountant may also be called upon to assist lawyers in the litigation process.

Information Technology Services

The growth in information technology has created many job opportunities for accountants with strong computer skills. There is a tremendous need for professionals who can design and implement advanced systems to fit a company's specialized needs. Accountants skilled in software research and development (including multimedia technology) are also highly valued.

International Accounting

Another prime growth area for CPAs is international accounting. Crossborder transactions are becoming commonplace, due in part to the dismantling of controlled economies in Eastern Europe and Latin America, the passage of the North American Free Trade Agreement (NAFTA) and the General Agreement on Tariffs and Trade (GATT), as well as economic growth in areas such as the Pacific Rim. Functional skills needed in a global economy include an understanding of international trade rules, accords, and laws; crossborder merger and acquisition issues; and foreign business customs, cultures, and procedures. Multilingual skills are important, especially Spanish and French.

Management Consulting Services

Accountants are often requested by their clients to offer objective advice and technical assistance about a variety of business situations. Some common consulting engagements might be computerizing a company's accounting and reporting function, projecting a company's growth, implementing an internal control system, facilitating mergers and acquisitions, assisting with production and marketing techniques, and providing general suggestions on improving overall operating procedures.

Personal Financial Planning

Accountants who are specialists in financial planning work with individuals and families to develop financial goals and help make these plans become reality. Personal financial planning includes helping clients better manage their money through debt reduction and expense control, developing investment strategies and asset allocation plans, tax consulting, insurance analysis and planning, retirement planning, and minimizing estate and gift tax burdens.

Tax Advisory Services

With the ever-changing tax laws and the growing complexity of business, tax professionals are involved in everything from preparing tax returns to reorganizing a multinational company's domestic and foreign operations in a manner that takes into consideration such factors as U.S. and foreign taxes, cash investments, dividends, and economic growth. The CPA tax specialist must deal with a variety of tax problems and opportunities in three primary areas of tax practice: tax consulting, tax compliance, and representation of clients before the Internal Revenue Service (IRS). In addition to supplying technical competence, the tax specialist must exercise good financial judgment and creativity in order to provide constructive solutions to complex tax problems. Therefore, a thorough understanding of the client's business, investment, and personal objectives is required, as well as a thorough understanding of the tax laws and their applications.

Industry

Accountants provide a broad array of services in the industrial sector.

Corporate Finance

Under this broad category, accountants and CPAs are responsible for analyzing a company's future financing needs, making presentations to and negotiating with banks and other investors, and managing an organization's cash and investments.

Financial Reporting

The financial accountant is responsible for accumulating and verifying the data required for the preparation of financial statements. Accountants are also often in charge of the design, implementation, and maintenance of the computer system used in the preparation of financial statements.

Internal Auditing

The CPA as internal auditor is responsible for providing an objective review of the company's financial and operating systems. She or he may also assist outside CPAs in their examination and evaluation of the company's financial statements. The internal auditor also functions as an in-house management consultant to senior management.

Management Accounting

Tax accountants working in management accounting are responsible for the accumulation and reporting of historical data in a format and level of detail required by management for making business decisions. Cost accounting and adherence to accounting theory are major responsibilities in this function.

Tax Planning

Accountants are responsible for determining the company's liability to various taxing authorities for income tax, licenses, sales tax, property tax, and payroll tax. They analyze the effects of tax accounting alternatives and study laws and regulations to ensure correct application of new tax measures.

Non-Financial Positions

Accountants are broad-based experts whose knowledge and skills are sought and valued by management in various non-financial positions. Accountants can succeed in business as top-level managers, chief executive officers, and company presidents.

Government/Not-For-Profit

The government and not-for-profit sectors also provide many career opportunities for accountants.

Government Accounting

Accountants in government have the opportunity to evaluate the efficiency of government departments and agencies at the federal, state, and local levels. At the federal level, accountants may be involved in testifying before a legislative committee on an audit or on the impact of pending tax legislation. At the state level, accountants may serve on a team assessing the adequacy of the investment portfolio of the treasurer's office.

Not-For-Profit Accounting

Accountants in not-for-profit organizations provide the information these institutions need to ensure that the benefits and services they provide do not exceed revenues. Whether an accountant is on the staff of a not-for-profit organization or serves in an advisory capacity, she or he can help the organization solve tax problems, set up an internal control system, budget resources, and prepare financial data for fund raising.

Education

As educators, accountants are members of the faculties of colleges of business administration, professional schools of accountancy, graduate schools of business, and community colleges. As accounting faculty members, accountants instruct students in interesting areas such as auditing, financial accounting, taxation, cost and managerial accounting, professional ethics, and many others. In addition to their teaching requirements, accountant educators conduct research to expand the body of accounting knowledge, and author books and articles on accounting theory.

INTEGRATION AND TRANSITION

To prepare for an accounting career you will need a solid technical accounting background that you will acquire in formal accounting courses. In addition, you will need a broad understanding of business and economics, which you will get from your business core courses and electives, and a good foundation in the humanities. Essential personal skills include creativity, the ability to solve problems, an understanding of business systems and computers, excellent communication skills, and high ethical standards.

You have examined four elements of the Recurring Themes model: communication and teamwork; economics; the business environment and ethics; and accounting. As you pursue your business education, you will find that these topics affect all business activities in all organizations. Chapter 6 will discuss another recurring theme that has already been alluded to: Information Systems and Computer Applications. That chapter also presents Quantitative Business Analysis as an essential skill in the successful operation of a business.

DISCUSSION AND ACTION

1. What is the role of accounting in the successful operation of a business?

2. What skills are needed to become a successful accountant?

3. Identify three types of professional accounting certification and the requirements for each.

4. Describe the general job opportunities that exist for accountants.

5. Identify and describe the specialties that exist within the public practice domain of the accounting profession.

6. Describe the specialties that exist within the private or industrial sector of accounting.

7. Describe job opportunities that exist within the government and not-for-profit sectors.

8. How do accountants help companies reach their goals?

9. Identify and interview an accountant who works for a local business, not-for-profit organization, or government agency. Ask the person to describe a typical working day. In a memorandum to your instructor, write a brief summary (one or two pages) of your findings.

10. Review your local newspaper or a business magazine. Find a story that illustrates the importance of accounting activities in a company. Bring the story to class for analysis and discussion.

11. Visit the Career Center on your campus. Find additional information about job opportunities for graduates with an accounting major. Be prepared to give a brief oral presentation (2–3 minutes) of your findings. Be selective as you prepare the presentation. Use the guides for business presentations given in Chapter 2.

12. Review the parts of the Recurring Themes model that have been discussed. Describe situations in which an accountant must apply communication and teamwork skills. In what ways will an understanding of economics and of the business environment help an accountant perform her or his duties more effectively?

REFERENCES

This chapter draws upon information available on the World Wide Web at AICPA.org. Used by permission of AICPA.

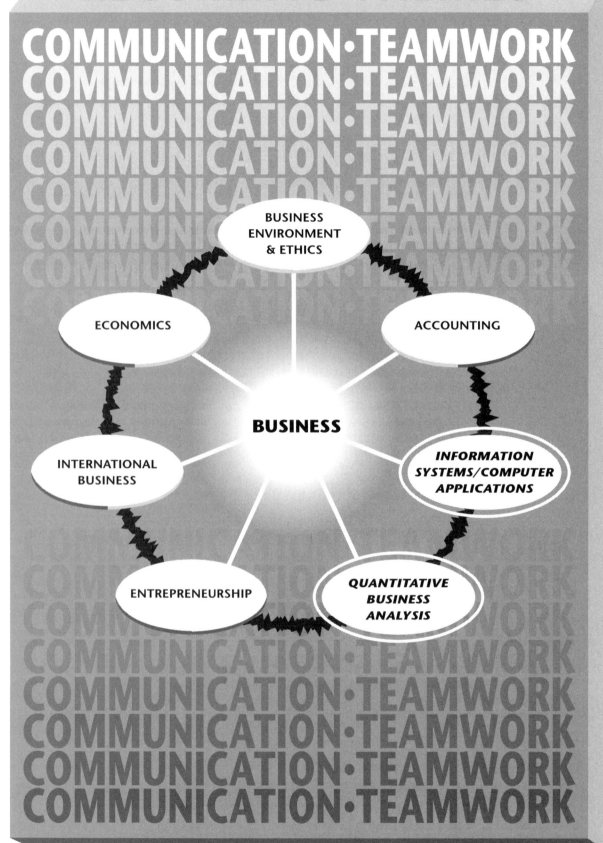

CHAPTER 6

INFORMATION SYSTEMS AND QUANTITATIVE BUSINESS ANALYSIS

OBJECTIVES

After you have read this chapter and completed related activities, you should be able to:

1. Distinguish between *data* and *information*.
2. Give examples of information systems at work in U.S. businesses.
3. Explore career opportunities in information systems.
4. Discuss the significance of quantitative business analysis for business today.
5. Explore career opportunities related to quantitative business analysis.

You have studied four elements of the Recurring Themes model: communication and teamwork, economics, the business environment, and accounting. This chapter considers two additional elements of the model: Management Information Systems/Computer Applications, and Quantitative Business Analysis.

As has been suggested in previous chapters, your ability to use a computer efficiently will have a significant impact on your career success. Moreover, some of the most exciting business developments and opportunities are occurring in the fields of management information systems (MIS) and quantitative business analysis (QBA), both of which rely heavily on computer applications. These fields offer several interesting avenues of study leading to rewarding, well-paying, and challenging careers.

This chapter first discusses the role of management information systems in business and then moves to a discussion of quantitative business analysis. The chapter concludes with a reminder that mastery of computer applications is essential not only for specialists in management information systems or quantitative business analysis, but for all employees in all areas of the organization.

THE INFORMATION AGE

The development of information as a major business resource and of information technology has been so dramatic that many social analysts label this the "information age." We have experienced the agricultural and industrial revolutions, and now find ourselves in the information revolution. From our homes to our businesses, from durable goods to intangible services, from our local community to the other side of the world, information is changing our lives. And the changes have just begun.

In addition, sophisticated and effective quantitative techniques are used increasingly in support of all business functions to make better business decisions. The rapid development of mathematical, logical, and statistical models, along with the almost unbelievable developments in computer hardware and software, have resulted in decision-making capabilities never dreamed of only a few years ago. The availability of data reflecting our experiences, coupled with the structure and power of decision-making models, has truly resulted in the application of scientific methods to business problems.

INFORMATION SYSTEMS

Ask several business people to identify what they believe to be one of the most dynamic areas affecting business today. Then, no matter what their field of expertise, ask them to pick out an area in which skills can greatly increase their effectiveness as a manager. You will find that many of them respond with "information systems" to both questions. Speedy communications, rapid transmission of data, the ability to process massive databases, access to tremendous information capabilities on your own desktop, linkage to global networks or networks within a small business—all these and other aspects of information systems can radically increase your effectiveness as a businessperson and improve the performance of your business. Understanding information systems can assure that all these blessings don't become a curse. Whether you are a specialist or an end-user, the management of information and the use of information technology will be vital in your first job and will probably become even more important as your career progresses.

Data versus Information

To understand information systems, you must distinguish between data and information. Data are raw facts and figures; information, on the other hand, is the meaningful, useful interpretation of data.

For example, consider these facts:

- Although persons aged 65 and older will make up only 13 percent of the U. S. population by the year 2000, that group is projected to grow as much as 58 percent between 2000 and 2030 (Campanelli, 1994).
- The 18–24 and 25–34 age groups are expected to decline 3 percent and 20 percent respectively between 2000 and 2030 (Campanelli, 1994).

- Between 1995 and 2050, the greatest increases in the 65-plus population will be in the Hispanic, Asian and Pacific Islander, and Native American ethnic groups (Campanelli, 1994).
- In 1996, 33 percent of persons age 50 and over lived in the Middle Atlantic and South Atlantic regions of the United States, and the effective buying power in those regions was 4.5 percent higher than the U.S. average (*Sales and Marketing Management,* 1996).

If all these data are put together in a meaningful way, they might produce information about the potential market for elder-care goods and services. The challenge for managers in industries such as clothing, food services, recreation, public transportation, insurance, housing, and health care is to turn masses of data into manageable information for decision making.

Management Information Systems

A management information system is the interaction of several elements to transform data into manageable information. Information systems involve people, software, hardware, communications networks, and data sources. Through the use of information technology and in interaction with the human manager, information systems collect data, process or transform data, and distribute information. In a business, all this activity should result in the creation of value for customers.

For example, when you buy a sweatshirt at your college bookstore, you trigger information systems activity. The information system includes recording and controlling the flow of information about that sweatshirt from the point of sale in the bookstore back through the storeroom, to the distribution center, into the factory, and even back to the supplier of raw materials. This flow of information increases the likelihood that the next time you want a sweatshirt, it will be available in the size, design, and color that you want. Other examples of information systems in operation include maintaining accurate data on the sale of stocks, bonds, and other financial instruments; tracking a marketing campaign; controlling a worldwide system of mail or package distribution; keeping track of the inventory in a small antiques store; marketing products electronically; and managing reservations, crew schedules, aircraft maintenance, and many other functions for a major airline.

Data pervade all areas and types of business. The need for people capable of converting data into information and managing and using that information can only grow. You can be sure that other individuals with whom you compete for jobs, and other businesses with which your business will compete, will fully recognize the importance of managing information.

An Undergraduate Information Systems Program

In some schools, a major in business information systems can be earned by taking 12 hours of prescribed course work. The 12 hours usually consist of one required course on business information systems and three courses selected from options such as quantitative methods for business, computer-based decision making for business, business systems design, business telecommunications, implementation of business information systems, simulation of business systems, or decision support and expert systems. This major is designed primarily for students who wish to acquire a basic understanding of the field. Typically, this major would enable the student to take a second major. Thus, the 12-hour major provides an opportunity for a broad-based business education, including higher computer and information literacy among all business students. Upon graduation, the student could begin work in a business area such as marketing, finance, or human resources, and make effective use of information systems knowledge to enhance her or his performance.

A more intensive major in business information systems usually requires at least 18 hours of prescribed course work. The intensive major is intended to meet the needs of students who have an interest in pursuing a career as an information systems professional. The required upper-division business courses in information systems cover the areas of conceptual foundations, systems, and data management to give the students a thorough grasp of the concepts, techniques, and methods of modern information systems development and technology management. The program usually requires as many as four courses covering business information systems, business systems design, business telecommunications, and business information structures and design. In addition, elective courses are selected from areas such as quantitative methods for business, computer-based decision making for business, implementation of business information systems, simulation of business systems, and decision support and expert systems.

Although a 12-hour information systems major does not require technical computer courses, students pursuing an intensive major would be wise to complete several credit hours of technical course work in areas such as computer programming, operating systems, object-oriented technologies and application development, networking technologies, distributed systems and database development, internet technologies, geographic information systems, and other technical aspects of information technology. If these courses are not offered in a department or school of business, a student should investigate the possibility of obtaining these courses through a minor outside of business. For example, the courses may be available in the department of computer science, applied technical sciences, or electrical and computer engineering.

Although such an "outside" minor would be valuable to any student who wishes to acquire basic knowledge and skill in applying information technology tools, it is particularly recommended for students taking an intensive major in business information systems. These non-business administration courses in information technology should provide the student with the necessary technical skills that are commonly regarded as essential for a career as an information systems professional. The business information systems courses emphasize high-level methodologies and managerial, strategic, and behavioral elements of information systems development; but ideally they should be complemented by the technical expertise provided by the non-business administration course work.

Career Opportunities in Information Systems

The job opportunities for information systems majors are excellent; the field is widely recognized for both current and future career potential. Any report of future employment opportunities stresses the tremendous growth of the information field. There will be explosive growth in the need for information systems; and because the success or failure of these systems depends on human expertise, the continuing and growing demand for capable people educated in information systems is assured.

Information systems majors are hired by a variety of businesses and governmental agencies that have extensive computer systems, or by data processing service firms and software developers. Opportunities range from large organizations to small businesses. Positions are available in functional areas of business such as manufacturing, marketing, and finance, or in staff areas such as corporate planning or information systems. In addition to other businesses, there are explosive opportunities in firms directly involved in information systems and technology, including hardware and software vendors and website developers. Many opportunities are also available in consulting firms. Some students are initially employed in the information systems part of an organization while others become the information systems specialist in a functional area, such as operations or marketing. In the latter case, duties may include providing liaison with the information systems area.

Positions for information systems majors range from programmer trainee to programmer/analyst to application programmer to systems analyst to end-user support specialist to manager of data processing and beyond. Naturally, the first position will depend heavily on factors such as the applicant's specific course of study and previous experience.

The work in an information systems position usually consists of some variation of applying information technology to business or government problems. For example, systems analysts may determine requirements and prepare specifications for an information system under development and devise solutions for problems that occur during the project. Systems analysts may also be involved in such diverse activities as new product development, customer service, consulting, records retention programs, cost-benefit feasibility studies, file utilization studies, and information systems for functional applications such as accounting, operations, and marketing.

A career in information systems will increasingly provide tremendous opportunities to progress into top management. More and more companies are not only depending on information systems as a support resource but as the basis for their product structure. A background in information systems is a great advantage in making the difficult management decisions faced by any organization.

The compensation for information systems positions has been consistently high, reflecting the number of job opportunities compared to the number of people being educated in this field and the importance of the field to hiring organizations. Salary figures can range widely and depend on total educational experience, work experience, region, industry, and size of firm.

Many students will choose to focus on a career path outside of information systems. For those individuals, some work in information systems can provide very significant career advantages.

As you can see, information systems clearly supports all activities of a firm. The need to manage information will appear as a theme in all the business courses that you take as you prepare for your career. Because of the complexity of business operations, you will also repeatedly hear about the necessity of applying quantitative tools in the analysis of business problems.

QUANTITATIVE BUSINESS ANALYSIS

Quantitative business analysis (QBA) focuses on scientific decision making and the scientific design and operation of business systems. It integrates the fields of mathematics and statistics with the power of the computer and supplements these with knowledge from other fields, such as marketing or finance, to help managers make better business decisions.

Although scientific methods have been used as an aid to management for many centuries, quantitative business analysis as a formal discipline has its roots in programs to improve military operations in World War II. After the war, many of the techniques that had been used for military problems found applications in business. Today, the use of quantitative business analysis is found in all areas of business including accounting, finance, marketing, information systems, and operations management.

Some of these applications include scheduling the production of goods or the provision of services; controlling inventories; conducting market segmentation and media allocation studies; drawing samples for surveys; conducting opinion polls; scheduling airline operations, including reservation systems; forecasting product demand; improving product and process quality; scheduling distribution systems; making financial decisions; planning staffing levels and developing staffing schedules; managing accounts receivable and cash flow; and managing large projects such as the construction of an office building. One of the most exciting aspects of quantitative business analysis is the diversity of business endeavors in which significant contributions can be made.

Even though the use of quantitative business analysis is often discussed in the context of large companies, the techniques are also useful for small business and even for personal decision making. For example, a network planning model sketched out on a legal pad can be very helpful in planning your next party.

An Undergraduate Program in Quantitative Business Analysis

Please note that some confusion can result from the many terms used to describe the field we call quantitative business analysis. As you seek information about QBA, whether in descriptions of academic programs or career opportunities, you may encounter some of these alternative titles: management science, operations research, decision sciences, decision analysis, quantitative methods, systems analysis, applied or business statistics, and many others.

In many schools, an initial course on the use of computers in business and one on statistics for business and economics are required of all business students. A major in quantitative business analysis requires at least an additional 12 credit hours of prescribed course work, with some of these courses being required and others being selected by students from several options. The required courses will provide a coverage of applied statistical modeling and quantitative models for business. Optional courses may cover advanced management science, forecasting and time series, statistical quality control, simulation of business systems, and the analysis of decisions under uncertainty.

Combining a major in quantitative business analysis with a second business administration major or concentrations from other business areas can provide a background that includes both a functional expertise and a particular strength in quantitative analysis. In addition, the careful selection of courses for a non-business administration minor can create an overall educational program that will enhance career opportunities. For example, additional courses in mathematics, statistics, or research design can complement a quantitative business analysis major.

Career Opportunities in Quantitative Business Analysis

Quantitative business analysis is a dynamic and rapidly-growing area. Graduates are employed in many positions, from general managers to statisticians and research analysts.

Students with training in quantitative business analysis are hired by many businesses and governmental agencies. Opportunities range from large organizations to small businesses. Manufacturing firms, transportation companies, overnight delivery services, banks, hospitals, and investment firms all use quantitative business analysis. For general management positions, training in quantitative business analysis will provide problem-solving techniques and ways of examining problems that will be of great help in making better managerial decisions. Those working in specialized quantitative analysis jobs will use various mathematical and statistical models in the analysis and solution of business problems. Examples of such problems include determining locations for new facilities, designing experiments to determine the effectiveness or acceptance of new products, designing quality control procedures, designing an efficient distribution system, developing a workforce schedule, or planning future production capacity.

A background in quantitative analysis is a great advantage in analyzing the problems faced by any organization. The manager with a good supporting knowledge in quantitative business analysis will be at an advantage when competing for top management positions. The increasing complexities of managing global competition also emphasizes the importance of quantitative analysis in decision making.

The first position that a QBA graduate takes will depend on many factors, including the student's specific course of study and previous experience. However, it is difficult to envision any career path where success would not be facilitated by the ability to apply the power of quantitative business analysis to the complex problems of today's organizations. Students who choose to focus on a career path other than quantitative business analysis will find that study of the field can still provide very significant career advantages.

The compensation for quantitative business analysis positions has been consistently high. This is a reflection of the importance of the field to hiring organizations compared to the number of people being prepared in this field. Salary figures can range widely and depend on total educational experience, work experience, region, industry, and size of firm.

COMPUTER APPLICATIONS

As you have seen from the descriptions of management information systems and quantitive business analysis, both fields depend heavily on computer expertise. The bottom line is that to function in today's business world, you must be familiar and comfortable with a broad range of computer software and hardware. Whether you are projecting the number of temporary employees needed to meet a major production deadline or computing the weekly payroll, assembling content for the company's annual report or preparing the final layout of the report, reporting your sales for a day or planning an international marketing campaign, you will use a computer. Although you may not need the expertise of the MIS or QBA specialist, you must become proficient in the use of the software and hardware associated with word processing and document design, database management, spreadsheet and statistical analysis, and graphics production. If you have not already developed such proficiency, now is a good time to begin.

INTEGRATION AND TRANSITION

As you review the Recurring Themes model, remind yourself again that many areas of knowledge support the successful operation of a firm, and information about those areas will be present to varying degrees in nearly every business course you take. This chapter has focused specifically on the themes of management information systems and quantitative business analysis, as well as the importance of mastering the basic computer applications that you will use daily on the job.

Complementing the business knowledge gained in other parts of the undergraduate program with the MIS and QBA skills provides a powerful business education. The skills gained through the study of management information systems and quantitative business analysis can be useful not only to the student who specializes in these areas but also to the student pursuing a career in another aspect of business.

Two recurring themes remain for analysis: Entrepreneurship and International Business. Chapter 7 introduces you to entrepreneurship in conjunction with a study of the management function in the firm. Chapter 11 will discuss how all themes and functional areas are brought together in the international business arena.

DISCUSSION AND ACTION

1. Explain the following terms:
   - data
   - information
   - information age
   - management information system
   - quantitative business analysis

2. In your judgment, how can a management information system give a company a competitive edge in a changing business environment?

3. How did quantitative business analysis get its start?

4. Is a management information systems or business information systems major available in your college? If so, what are the requirements for that major?

5. Is a quantitative business analysis major available in your college? If so, what are the requirements for that major?

6. Locate a person in your community whose major job responsibilities are in the MIS or QBA areas. Interview that person; or if the person agrees to respond to an e-mail message, obtain the information by e-mail. In a memorandum to your instructor, summarize the results of the interview. Use the following questions to guide your interview.

   • When and how did you develop an interest in this type of career?

   • Where did you get the necessary education for the position you now hold?

   • What are your major job responsibilities?

   • What courses, other than MIS or QBA courses, have helped you in your career?

   • Please describe a typical working day in this position.

7. Identify one area of computer applications in which you think you need additional skill. Find out where or how you can develop that skill. In a memo to your instructor, write an action plan to improve your computer skills.

8. Visit the Career Center on your campus. Find additional information about job opportunities for graduates with a major in management information systems or quantitative business analysis. Be prepared to give a brief oral presentation (2–3 minutes) of your findings. Be selective as you prepare the presentation. Use the guides for business presentations given in Chapter 2.

REFERENCES

CAMPANELLI, M. (1994). Selling to seniors: A waiting game. *Sales & Marketing Management*, 146, June, p. 69.

Supplement (1996). *Sales & Marketing Management*, 148, June, p. 54.

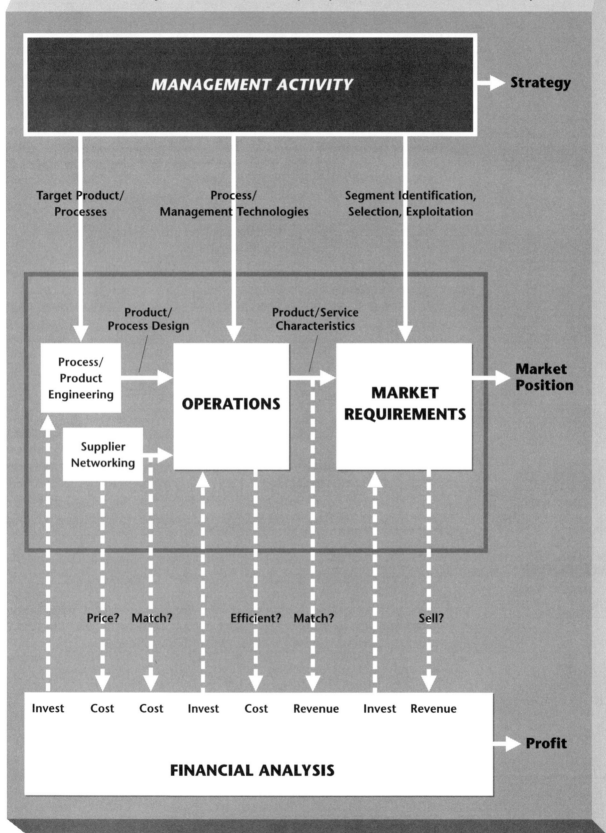

CHAPTER 7

MANAGEMENT

OBJECTIVES

After you have read this chapter and completed related activities, you should be able to:

1. Discuss the fundamental tasks of the management function in a firm.

2. Identify and describe the five management functions in which managers engage.

3. Identify and describe four core management skills that a person must have to be an effective manager.

4. Identify typical specialties within the management area that may be available to students.

5. Begin to explore career options and opportunities in management.

Because the management function is an umbrella that covers the entire organization, it appears at the top of the Business Function Integration model. This chapter describes several things about management as it relates to you as a business student. First, it suggests some reasons to study management. Second, it provides an overview of some basic management fundamentals. Third, it describes the management courses that you will take as a business student, regardless of your major or area of concentration. Fourth, it describes the management program area in the typical school of business and three specialties within that area. Fifth, it provides some basic information about typical undergraduate concentrations that are available within the broad area of management. The chapter concludes with a brief discussion of what makes management exciting, frustrating, and interesting, but never, never boring!

WHY STUDY MANAGEMENT?

Today it seems that everyone is an expert on management. Bookstores are filled with books on the topic: *Thriving on Chaos, Swim with the Sharks Without Being Eaten Alive, The One Minute Manager, Managing Takes More Than a Minute*. News media regularly cite so-called management experts on one topic or another. These topics can range from statements by current or former Chief Executive Officers, professional basketball coaches, retired Army generals, and popular cartoonists.

Most of us have had experience as employees, which means that we also have had the experience of being managed. We may like the manner in which our manager carries out her or his duties, or we may hate it; but few of us are too shy to offer an opinion about what constitutes good or bad management. Why, for example, have the "Dilbert" cartoons become so popular? In large part, their popularity can be attributed to Adams's regular attacks on "bad" management; that is, the boss who just "doesn't get it" or who takes gleeful delight in "sticking it" to the employees. Are all managers as bad as the horn-haired manager in the Dilbert cartoons? Of course not, but most of us laugh because we have endured—or have at least heard about—experiences just like those that Mr. Adams satirizes.

Management is often defined in terms of various functions, such as planning, organizing, staffing, directing, and controlling. These management functions assist the organization in carrying out its objectives in the most effective and efficient manner possible (Skinner and Ivancevich, 1996). In its very essence, though, *management* has to do with the management of people. Management is carried out by one or more managers for the purpose of getting things done through other people. The focus is not so much on managing numbers or managing raw materials, but on managing people.

The primary rationale for studying management is the following: *Management is ubiquitous!* This is just a fancy way of saying that management is everywhere. Every active member of society is influenced by management in some way. If you work for a Fortune 500 corporation, a strong management framework is in place. If you work in a small organization, there is at least one manager, namely the owner. If you work for the government, you will encounter plenty of management. And if you work for a not-for-profit organization such as the Peace Corps or a religious order, management is there too. In addition, many of you will become managers in the future, and some of you already are managers in your current jobs. You may start your career in a functional specialization, such as accounting, marketing, or information systems, but will be promoted into management as your career progresses.

SOME FUNDAMENTALS OF MANAGEMENT

The discipline of management deals with setting objectives, understanding and applying the management functions, and developing core management skills. Many of your experiences as a college student are applications of management theory to your personal and academic life.

Objectives

Organizations exist for some purpose. Some examples include, "to make a profit for the shareholders of our business," "to protect the natural environment of our state," "to promote healthy eating habits in our children," and "to provide for the physical and spiritual needs of the homeless." Whether run for profit or as a not-for-profit organization, an organization needs overall objectives that guide and direct the actions of its members. These objectives should be linked to the organization's mission statement, which describes the purpose, scope, and uniqueness of the organization. A well-done mission statement clearly communicates the vision of the organization and provides a focus as to what the organization is all about.

When done right, an organization's strategic planning process results in a clear sense of the organizational mission and clear-cut objectives. These organizational objectives then serve as a catalyst for objectives within the departments of the organization. The departmental objectives can in turn guide the objectives for various subunits, such as work teams, quality improvement teams, or special-project teams. Finally, objectives for individual employees should be linked in a clear and measurable way to the objectives set at all higher levels.

Management Functions

Once objectives have been set, a major role of managers is to assist in accomplishing these objectives. Since the early part of the twentieth century, management theorists such as Henri Fayol, Mary Parker Follett, and Chester Barnard have identified a number of primary functions that managers perform. Still today, five functions describe a large portion of what managers do in their jobs. These functions are planning, organizing, staffing, directing, and controlling.

Planning

Planning is deciding in advance what needs to be done (Skinner and Ivancevich, 1996). Effective planning requires determining who will do what job, how long a job will take, and what resources are needed to get the job done. Although planning takes much time and energy and can involve complex decision making, planning is essential to help an organization remain competitive in today's fast-paced business environment. Many of the business declines and failures of the past decades can be attributed to inadequate planning. A popular management expression is: "The person who fails to plan, plans to fail." Planning issues are a major focus of strategic management classes.

Organizing

Organizing has to do with the way in which organizations are structured to carry out their plans and objectives. It concerns the type of hierarchy and reporting relationships within an organization, as well as the technology and physical plant used to carry out the organization's objectives. Organizing issues are addressed most heavily in classes on organizational behavior and organizational theory.

Staffing

Staffing refers to the selection, development, appraisal, and compensation of employees. Irving Shapiro, retired CEO of DuPont, has said, "The greatest satisfaction is being able to identify talent and develop it and get people into positions where their talents can be used constructively" (Megginson, et al., 1992). Although staffing activities are most often thought of as human resource management functions, they are nonetheless clearly important functions of general management. Staffing issues are emphasized in human resource management courses.

Directing

Directing has to do with initiating action; that is, issuing directives, making assignments, and giving instructions. Directing is closely related to leadership. Much effort has been expended seeking to understand the qualities or styles of effective leaders. For example, how much of the success of Wal-Mart can be attributed to the leadership style of founder Sam Walton and his love of interaction with floor-level employees? These sorts of issues are addressed in almost all management classes, but are most heavily emphasized in organizational behavior classes.

Controlling

Controlling is making sure that planned performance is actually carried out. It requires a considerable amount of assessment and measurement. Performance standards must be established, and the methods to measure performance must be determined. Performance must then be measured and compared to the standard, and corrective actions must be taken when necessary. Monitoring is an essential aspect of this process, and today an increasing number of these control and measurement functions are being pushed down to lower levels in the organization. Although managers must ensure that these controlling functions are being carried out, managers are less likely than in the past to be personally involved in such activities. Controlling and assessment functions are discussed in most management classes and are also heavily emphasized in classes offered in management science, information systems, or operations management.

Core Management Skills

Core management skills are the knowledge, behaviors, and aptitudes required to be an effective manager. While those skills obviously vary—depending upon whether one is a manager of an owner-operated small business or a manager at the lower, middle, or upper levels of a large organization—recent research suggests that four core management skills are required of all managers (Skinner and Ivancevich, 1996):

- decision making and problem solving skills
- communication skills
- interpersonal skills
- goal setting skills

Decision making and problem solving skills involve identifying problems, creating and evaluating alternatives, selecting an optimal alternative, and delegating aspects of the decision making process. Communication skills include written and oral communication, computer competence, and effective listening. Interpersonal skills include the ability to resolve conflict, show empathy, lead effectively, and behave in an ethical manner. Finally, goal setting skills include establishing objectives that are clear, challenging, and meaningful for all organizational members; setting priorities; evaluating success in goal achievement; and properly rewarding employees for their contributions to successful goal achievement.

MANAGEMENT AND THE BUSINESS CORE

Most students who earn undergraduate degrees in business administration must take a set of core business courses. This core usually includes a minimum of two courses taught by the management program area. The first course, often entitled Principles of Management or something similar, is generally required during the second or third year of business studies. The course gives an overview of the field of management, including an introduction to some topics taught by other areas, such as management science or operations management. The second course is usually required during the last year of study. It goes by titles such as Business Policy, Strategic Management, or Integrated Business Studies. This course is designed as the capstone course for your undergraduate business education and seeks to integrate your learning from all previous business courses in your curriculum. It asks questions concerning how organizations develop competitive advantages over other organizations, and why some organizations prosper while others do not.

Most students will also take a basic course in business or professional communication, either as a core requirement or as an elective. Business communication courses may be offered by the management area or by another department, such as English, Marketing, or Information Systems. The role of communication in business, and in your business education, was discussed in Chapter 2.

THE MANAGEMENT PROGRAM AREA

The management area is one academic discipline within a larger department or school of business. In larger universities the management department may offer a Bachelor of Science degree in management, with specializations or majors in areas such as organizational management, entrepreneurship, or human resource management.

The faculty of the management area often have diverse educational backgrounds, research interests, and teaching specialties. Their interests may include topics such as career issues, entrepreneurship, top management teams, work values, and fairness in the workplace. Management faculty typically maintain close contacts with the business community and enrich their teaching by bringing their research and their real-world business expertise into the classroom.

Five primary areas of interest are often found within the management program area. They are organizational behavior, human resource management, strategic management, entrepreneurship, and business communication.

Organizational Behavior

As a field of study, organizational behavior seeks to understand and manage human behavior within the work context. The emphasis can be on individual employees, work groups, or the organization as a whole. Some of the theoretical questions addressed by researchers in this area include the following:

- What motivates employees to attain high levels of performance?
- What factors (rational or otherwise) influence the way in which individuals make decisions?
- What can organizations do to manage intergroup conflict and organizational politics?
- What constitutes effective leadership?
- How can organizations be designed to promote organizational effectiveness?

Students will be exposed to some of this material in the principles of management course; in addition, many colleges offer interested students a more comprehensive course entitled Organizational Behavior.

Human Resource Management

Within the management discipline, another specialty area emphasizes human resource management and industrial relations. Human resource management can be viewed as a more applied or practical subfield within organizational behavior. Human resource management seeks to improve how organizations recruit, select, train, appraise, and compensate their employees. Industrial relations places particular emphasis on labor unions and the collective bargaining process between management and organized labor.

Strategic Management

Another major area within the management discipline is the strategy or strategic management area. Strategic management asks the questions, "Why do organizations differ from one another?" and "How does management influence overall organizational performance?" Some further theoretical questions addressed by researchers in this area include the following:

- How do organizations develop business strategies to compete in a particular industry?
- Are there general competitive strategies that are effective across various product markets and industries?
- Why do firms diversify?

- What types of organizational structures work best for particular organizational strategies?
- How do organizations best respond and adapt to changes in the world around them?

Students usually study these issues in depth in the strategic management course taken in their last semester of study.

Other faculty interests within the strategic management area include organizational theory and business ethics. Organizational theory addresses questions concerning the nature and structure of organizations and how organizations influence and are influenced by their environments. Business ethics, as the name implies, addresses the myriad ethical issues and dilemmas facing organizations and their managers.

Entrepreneurship

Within the management area, a growing number of programs offer courses that emphasize issues pertaining to small businesses and entrepreneurship. The past decade has seen a tremendous growth in the number of new business start-ups. Owner-managed and other smaller organizations have been hailed as increasingly critical to the growth of the U. S. economy. For example, in the early 1990s, it was estimated that over 90 percent of all job growth occurred in companies employing fewer than 100 workers (Richman, 1993).

Entrepreneurship courses stress, among other things, the importance of creative thinking and the willingness to assume risk. Moreover, the Recurring Themes model suggests that in a dynamic, rapidly-changing business environment, those entrepreneurial qualities are critical to the success of all organizations.

Business Communication

Management theorists have recognized that management of human resources and implementation of strategic plans requires effective communication. Further, a number of surveys have shown a positive relationship between communication skills and upward mobility in organizations. As argued by Andrews and Herschel (1996), these surveys point to "a variety of factors or skills, but all stress the importance of communicating effectively. . . . Moreover, when the skills or characteristics are ranked, communication competencies are invariably near the top."

Therefore, many management departments have also assumed the responsibility of helping students improve their business communication skills. Faculty members in this area specialize in effective professional communication, including the abilities to write effectively and make business presentations utilizing the latest in computer technology. Business communication courses may include a basic course in business communication and specialized courses that provide more intensive study of business report writing, business and professional speech, managerial communication, and document design.

UNDERGRADUATE MANAGEMENT MAJORS

Majors or areas of concentration that may be available within the Bachelor of Science degree in Management vary among colleges and universities, depending on school size and faculty expertise. Some typical majors and sample courses are listed in Table 7-1. Notice that some majors or areas of concentration may include courses (such as finance, accounting, marketing research) that complement courses normally thought of as management courses. If you are interested in any of the suggested majors, be sure to check the specific requirements of your college.

Table 7-1

Undergraduate Management Majors

Major or Concentration	Sample Courses
Business Communication	Business Communication (sometimes called Business Writing or Professional Communication) Business Report Writing Organizational Behavior Managerial Communication Document Design
Entrepreneurship	Initiation and Management of New Business Enterprise Advanced Issues in Entrepreneurship Human Resource Management Principles of Marketing Research Intermediate Finance Cost/Managerial Accounting Managerial Economics International Marketing
Human Resource Management	Human Resource Management Organizational Behavior Advanced Human Resource Management Industrial Relations Business Communication
Organizational (General) Management	Organizational Behavior Organizational Theory Advanced Organizational Behavior Human Resource Management Business Communication

MANAGEMENT IS FUN, MANAGEMENT IS FRUSTRATING . . .

What this short chapter has tried to communicate is that management is an exciting, dynamic topic. To be an effective member of a business or a not-for-profit organization, you will need to understand the goals and aims of management. You will also need to relate effectively to the managers under whose supervision you will work. Furthermore, whether by design or by default, many of you will become managers yourselves in the future. This will require particular skills and abilities to carry out your job, whatever that may be.

If you accept the idea that management is the process of accomplishing things through people, then you can also see why it is simultaneously both interesting and frustrating. Some people are as firm and dependable as the Rock of Gibraltar; others are unreliable. Sometimes even good employees make errors, develop personal problems, or get into trouble with the law. In spite of the increasing amount of science that has accumulated about management, there is still a good portion of art connected to the practice of management. Therefore, nobody has all the answers: not Michael Eisner at Disney; not the latest "management guru" with a paid infomercial on television; and not even the professors in your management program!

What you should obtain from the management program is the latest and most relevant information concerning topics that will matter to you in your future career. You will also develop skills and acquire tools that you will need to succeed personally. You are urged to check out the courses and concentrations available in the management area of your college. Regardless of your interests or ultimate major, you will be well-served by the types of problem solving, communication, and planning skills that you will develop in the various management courses.

A FINAL CAVEAT

You might have noticed that this chapter does not describe job opportunities for undergraduate majors. Here is the plain truth on the matter. For entrepreneurship majors and anyone else interested in starting a business, the sky is the limit. There are plenty of opportunities out there; but these opportunities generally take plenty of capital, lots of hard work, and a fair amount of serendipity or good fortune. Even so, a fairly high percentage of business start-ups fail. So, entrepreneurship is not for the faint of heart. If you are highly averse to risk, you might not want to become an entrepreneur.

If you are interested in human resource management, you should be aware that many human resource positions require a master's degree, and many smaller companies promote from within for HR positions. Students with an undergraduate degree in human resources management often begin in general management. Although there are human resource jobs available for undergraduate majors, they are not plentiful; you will have to go after them. Recruiters may not always come to campus looking for you.

This caveat is not intended to discourage you from taking management courses beyond the principles of management and business strategy that may be required in your program. Many students find that the study of organizational behavior, communication, and entrepreneurship are excellent complements to other business majors, such as finance or accounting. The chapters on those subjects will present specific career opportunities for accounting or finance majors. But the reality is that anyone who hopes to advance within a career must have an understanding of human behavior and communication. Opportunities to study those generally useful subjects are provided by the typical management department.

At the master's level, it is a different story. A student in a Master's of Human Resources (MHR) program, such as that offered at the University of South Carolina, may obtain a paid summer internship, which often leads to a job offer. In recent years, placement of MHR students has been strong, with excellent starting salaries. If you are serious about a career in Human Resources, you'd probably be best served by taking courses that develop your communication skills (oral, written, and computer). Also be sure to develop your analytical skills, especially skills in statistical analysis. Human Resources may be a "people profession," but the most successful managers of human resources also possess strong analytical skills.

INTEGRATION AND TRANSITION

You now have examined six topics from the Recurring Themes model and one from the Business Function Integration model. This chapter emphasized the importance of management in all organizations, and specific areas of study that will prepare people for general management positions. As you will see in the remaining chapters, however, every sector of the firm requires competent managers. Therefore, even if your major interest is in accounting, finance, or marketing, you will benefit by understanding and applying basic principles of management.

By now you should begin to understand that no individual or unit within an organization can operate independently. Although creative thought and risk-taking (entrepreneurial thinking) are significant in all operations, no successful firm can condone independent and fragmented thought or action.

The next chapter focuses on operations and its significance in a fully-integrated firm.

DISCUSSION AND ACTION

1. What is the role of management in business and not-for-profit organizations?
2. What is the purpose of managerial objectives? Give an example of a managerial objective.
3. Identify the five functions of management. Give an example of each as it applies to your life as a first-year college student.
4. Assume that you must collaborate with another student to write a one-page report for this class. The topic of the report is "How Management Functions Apply to My College Life." How will you apply the core management skills (as identified and discussed in this chapter) to complete that assignment successfully?
5. Identify specific management courses that are required in the business curriculum at your college.
6. Identify a faculty member in your college who teaches courses or conducts research in one of the areas of management (Organizational Behavior, Human Resources Management, Strategic Management,

Entrepreneurship, Business Communication). Interview that professor and report the results of the interview in a 5-minute presentation to your class. The following questions may guide your interview:

- When did you first become interested in this area? Why did you become interested?
- What kind of business or consulting experience related to this specialty have you had?
- What undergraduate or graduate courses do you teach? What is the major focus of each course? Who should take the course?
- What advice would you give to a student who is considering a career in this area?

7. Which of the areas within the management area interest you as a possible major or concentration? Why? If no area interests you, why is none interesting?

8. Visit the Career Center on your campus. Find additional information about job opportunities for graduates with a management major (or a major in one of the areas within management as described in this chapter). Be prepared to give a brief oral presentation (2–3 minutes) of your findings. Be selective as you prepare for the presentation. Give the most interesting data that you find.

REFERENCES

ANDREWS, P. H., and R. T. HERSCHEL (1996). *Organizational communication: Empowerment in a technological society*. Boston: Houghton Mifflin, p. 17

MEGGINSON, L. C., D. C. MOSLEY, and P. H. PIETRI, JR. (1992). *Management: Concepts and applications* 4th ed. New York: Harper Collins.

RICHMAN, L. S. (1993). Jobs that are growing and slowing. *Fortune*, 128, July 12, p. 53.

SKINNER, S. I., and J. M. IVANCEVICH (1996). *The business environment*. Cincinnati: South-Western College Publishing.

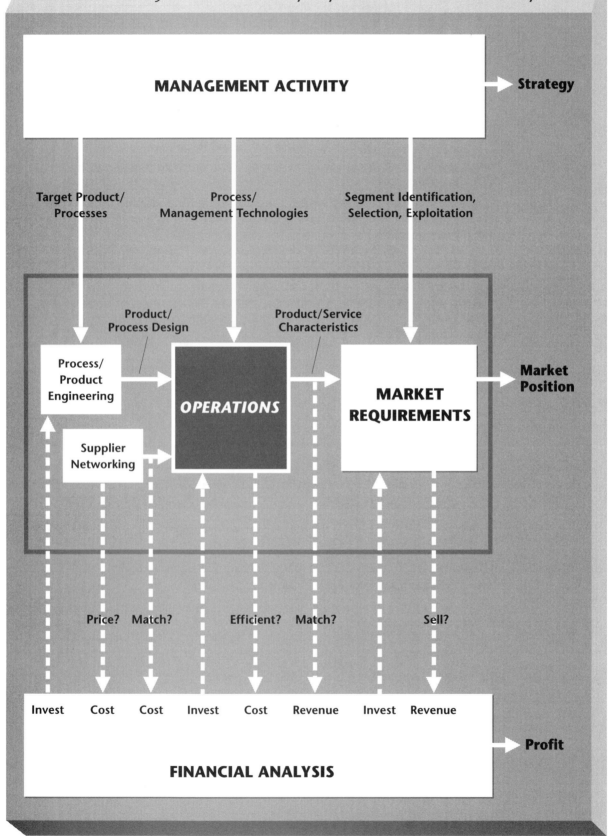

CHAPTER 8

OPERATIONS MANAGEMENT

OBJECTIVES

After you have read this chapter and completed related activities, you should be able to:

1. Describe the significance of the operations function in a business.

2. Describe how operations management differs from, or is similar to, general management.

3. Identify how to prepare for a career in operations management.

4. Begin to explore career opportunities in operations management.

Some of the most exciting business developments and opportunities today are occurring in the fields of information systems, quantitative business analysis, and operations management. These fields offer several interesting avenues of study leading to rewarding, well-paid, and challenging careers. The Recurring Themes model and Chapter 6 introduced you to the significance of information systems and quantitative business analysis as areas that undergird all operations. This chapter and the Business Function Integration model focus on the role of operations management as a major function in all firms—a function that must be integrated with other functions to achieve a successful, profitable business.

This chapter first explains the operations function in a firm. Second, it describes a typical undergraduate program in operations management and links an operations management program to information systems and quantitative business analysis. Finally it introduces career opportunities for operations management majors.

OPERATIONS MANAGEMENT

All businesses have faced tremendous changes in the competitive environment. Those that win are simply providing better goods and services. That is the function of operations—actually providing goods and services, and winning by managing suppliers, people, technology, and other resources better than competitors. Thus, there is an increasing recognition of the importance of managing operations to prosper in global competition. Whether occurring in a small company in South Carolina or in a large world-spanning corporation, operations are truly a core function of business and a competitive weapon vital to business success.

Operations is the part of an organization that produces its products, whether they be goods or services. The major elements of operations that must be managed are the inputs to the operating system (including raw materials, human resources, technology, and capital); the outputs of the system (physical goods or services); and the transformation process that converts the inputs into the outputs. Businesses universally recognize the importance of their processes that create customer value, and it is in those processes that many management challenges are found. Operations management focuses on those challenges.

There are a tremendous number of activities that must be performed within the framework of operations management. These include developing operations strategies; forecasting product demand; developing new products (goods or services); designing and managing the processes that create the products; making capacity decisions; deciding on the location of facilities; planning the physical layouts for the operating systems; designing jobs; developing production and staffing plans; scheduling operations; controlling inventory; managing large projects such as the construction of a shopping mall; providing quality assurance and control; planning and controlling logistics; and managing the supply chain.

The operations function is increasingly being recognized as a vital capability that is critical to success in global competition. This recognition has been slow in coming, which is a partial explanation for the problems experienced by many companies throughout the world. Delivering high-quality products and services quickly, reliably, and at low cost is critical for survival. Improvements in the competitive capabilities of business organizations, large and small, require individuals who can effectively and efficiently manage the operations function. Good marketing and tight financial controls are not enough. Those who can successfully manage operations are critical to success. It is also vital that corporate executives as well as managers in other functional areas of business understand the importance of operations to the success of their organizations. The demands of today's markets make understanding and cooperation among the diverse units of business absolutely necessary.

AN UNDERGRADUATE PROGRAM IN OPERATIONS MANAGEMENT

In many schools, a first course in operations management is a part of the business core. A major in operations management will require an additional 12 to 18 credit hours of prescribed course work. Some of those courses are required and others may be selected from several options. The required courses usually provide coverage of computer-based decision making for business, the management of logistics systems, and production and inventory control. Optional courses offer the student an opportunity to study quantitative methods for business, forecasting and time series, statistical quality control, and the simulation of business systems.

Operations combined with a second business administration major or concentrations from other business areas can provide a particularly strong background. In addition, the careful selection of non-business administration courses can create an overall educational program that will serve the student well in a future career in operations.

Many students will choose to focus on a career path outside of operations. However, for those individuals, some work in operations can be of great help in understanding a major functional area of business, and this understanding can provide very significant career advantages.

Some common threads, in addition to academic content, run through the study of operations management and the areas of management information systems or quantitative business analysis, which were presented in Chapter 6. For one thing, they are all closely linked to computer technology and quantitative analysis. Because of those common threads, some colleges house MIS, QBA, and operations within a single academic unit, sometimes called management science. In such colleges, students have considerable latitude in designing a program of study that includes one or more of the management science specializations. Alternatives include the selection of major areas and the courses within those areas, the customization of any of several concentrations, the pairing of two management science majors or of a management science major with another business major, and almost unlimited options in selecting courses from those offered as part of the non-BA component of the undergraduate program in business.

The discussions in this chapter and Chapter 6 concentrated on majors in operations, business information systems, and quantitative business analysis. Keep in mind, however, that whether as a major, a concentration, or a set of courses selected to complement your other academic interests, management science can help you prepare for the future.

CAREER OPPORTUNITIES IN OPERATIONS MANAGEMENT

Job opportunities for operations management majors are excellent both in numbers of jobs and in salaries. Since all organizations have an operations component, operations management majors are hired by a variety of businesses and governmental agencies. Opportunities range from large organizations to small businesses and include rapidly-growing openings in consulting firms. Positions are available in functional areas of business, such as manufacturing, service operations, marketing, and finance, or in staff areas, such as corporate planning and systems analysis.

Students specializing in operations management will find employment opportunities in a host of organizations including both manufacturing and service companies. In manufacturing these positions include production facility management, production planning and scheduling, master planning and scheduling, logistics and purchasing management, materials analysis, inventory control, quality control, and production supervision. In the service sector there is rapid job growth in numerous areas including banking, health care, the environment, distribution centers, and retail chains. Opportunities for operations managers are also found in project management and technical sales. Efficient operations are vital to any firm; so these jobs provide individuals both responsibilities and commensurate opportunities. Naturally, an entry-level position will depend on many factors, such as the student's specific course of study and previous experience.

Many members of top management started their careers in operations. Operations represent such a vital factor in organizational success and so many of the assets of organizations are invested in operations that it is no surprise that accomplishments are rewarded with advancement and additional responsibility. A successful record in operations provides an ideal background for the tough management decisions that must be made by today's business leaders.

The compensation for operations management positions has been consistently high reflecting the number of job opportunities available and the importance of the field to hiring organizations. Salary figures can range widely and depend on total educational experience, work experience, region, industry, and size of firm.

INTEGRATION AND TRANSITION

Specializations in MIS, QBA, or operations management provide entry to jobs that will interest and excite you, jobs of great variety that will challenge you each day. They all provide access to careers where you can be financially rewarded for your work. Perhaps of greatest importance, they provide an opportunity to make a difference. Whether you help provide a needed consumer product of high quality at a reasonable price or find a way to deliver health-care services to more of those who need them, you can make life better for others. The chance to make a contribution, to be stimulated by your work, and to be rewarded for your efforts are just a few of the reasons to consider a career in information systems, quantitative business analysis, or operations management.

Most exciting is the contemplation of what lies over the horizon in these fields; all will have an expanding role in the new millennium. Information systems, quantitative business analysis, and operations offer opportunities today and into the future; and they are all available to you, the student of business.

Previous chapters have focused your attention on the Recurring Themes model, leading through a consideration of several elements that support all business functions and help to integrate them. Those elements are communication and teamwork, economics, the business environment and business ethics, accounting, management information systems / computer applications, quantitative business analysis, and the entrepreneurial spirit. Chapters 7 and 8 have introduced you to two functional areas of business, management and operations, which appear in the Business Function Integration model. Chapter 9 presents another functional area, marketing, which must be integrated with the other functions to ensure a successful business endeavor.

DISCUSSION AND ACTION

1. What is the role of the operations function in an organization?
2. Refer to the Recurring Themes model. In what ways do the elements identified in the model contribute to the operations of a firm?
3. Identify the requirements for an operations management major or minor at your college.
4. Consider your college as a production system. Identify the following elements in the system:
   - Its external stakeholders
   - Its internal stakeholders
   - Its inputs
   - Its outputs
   - Some of the operations necessary to convert inputs into outputs
   - Its general managers
   - Its operations managers
5. Interview a faculty member who teaches operations management courses in your college. In a memorandum to your instructor, report the results of your interview. Use these questions, and others that are approved by your instructor, to guide the interview.
   - How long have you taught in this area?
   - What first attracted you to operations?
   - What is your major research emphasis?
   - What advice would you give to a student who is interested in operations management?
7. Which of the areas within management science (operations, MIS, or QBA) most interest you as a possible major or concentration? Why? If no area interests you, why do you not find them interesting?
8. Visit the Career Center on your campus. Find additional information about job opportunities for a student with an operations management major. Be prepared to give a brief oral presentation (2–3 minutes) of your findings. Be selective as you prepare for the presentation. Follow the guides for presentations given in Chapter 2.

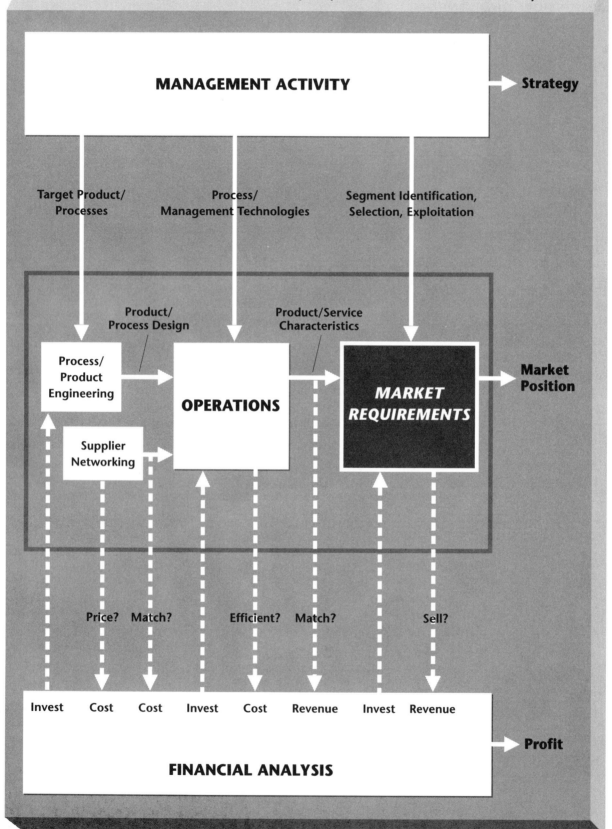

BUSINESS FUNCTION INTEGRATION
Functional activity viewed from the perspective of the whole enterprise.

MANAGEMENT ACTIVITY → **Strategy**

Target Product/ Processes

Process/ Management Technologies

Segment Identification, Selection, Exploitation

Product/ Process Design

Product/Service Characteristics

Process/ Product Engineering

OPERATIONS

MARKET REQUIREMENTS → **Market Position**

Supplier Networking

Price? Match? Efficient? Match? Sell?

Invest Cost Cost Invest Cost Revenue Invest Revenue

FINANCIAL ANALYSIS → **Profit**

CHAPTER 9

MARKETING

OBJECTIVES

After you have read this chapter and completed related activities, you should be able to:

1. Describe the function of marketing and its relationship to other functional units in the firm.

2. Identify broad career areas within marketing.

3. Describe how to prepare for a career in marketing.

This morning you probably showered, got dressed, ate breakfast, watched TV or listened to the radio, gathered your books, and then drove or walked to class. Chances are you shampooed your hair with Aveda or Head and Shoulders; selected Kellogg's Pop Tarts, Cheerios, or some other item for breakfast; donned your Levi's or your GAP jeans; put your books in an Eastpak or Jansport backpack; and, if you live off campus, drove a vehicle such as a Honda or Jeep Cherokee to campus.[1] Although you probably gave little thought to your specific consumption actions this morning, all of these choices were important to you when you made the purchase—at the grocery store, mall, bookstore, or car dealership. In fact, marketing is so important that it affects virtually everything we do.

As the Business Function Integration model demonstrates, marketing is one of the vital functions of a firm; it acts in harmony with management, operations, and finance. In this chapter you will learn about the broad spectrum of marketing and how it is related to the other functional areas of the firm. You will also be introduced to career options within marketing and how to prepare yourself for the marketing career of your choice.

MARKETING: IT'S ALL AROUND US

Most people are familiar with some aspects of marketing. Advertising and sales are the activities most closely associated with marketing; however, they are only a part of marketing's subject matter and practice. The field is much broader and includes such functions as product design, packaging decisions, distribution issues, pricing strategies, marketing-oriented public relations and sales promotions, and advertising and selling. Essentially, marketing affects almost every aspect of a business's operations. From designing the product to closing the sale, marketing research, planning, and strategy are used to guide a product or service through the process.

With such terms as *product design* and *pricing strategy*, you might think that marketing applies only to large corporations. On the contrary; large and small companies, business-to-consumer and business-to-business firms alike, market themselves and their products. Service firms, like doctors, lawyers, dentists, accountants, and dry cleaners, require marketing to succeed. Whether their marketing responsibilities are coordinated in-house or hired out to agencies, marketing is utilized to some degree by every type of business.

Not-for-profit organizations also market their offerings. For example, the American Red Cross uses public service announcements to recruit blood donors. Even the United States government markets its services, such as when the United States Postal Service urges consumers to buy new stamp issues upon their release. Colleges and universities use marketing when they recruit students. Remember that admissions counselor who spoke at College Night or conducted your campus tour? Cities and states also undertake marketing activities. The slogan "Columbia—A Capital Place to Be" is used to entice new residents to Columbia, South Carolina; and states lure tourists with advertising campaigns beginning with phrases like "Smiling Faces, Beautiful Places" in South Carolina, "Virginia is for lovers," or "Texas— It's Like a Whole Other Country." Politicians utilize marketing research to plan strategies to defeat their opponents and then develop media campaigns to inform and persuade voters to put them in office. Even the military uses marketing when it advertises to recruit inductees. So, as you can see, marketing is a prevalent force in our society.

What Exactly is Marketing?

Marketing is a common word and a ubiquitous practice, but what exactly does marketing mean? The American Marketing Association defines *marketing* as the process of planning and executing the conception, pricing, promotion, and distribution of ideas, goods, and services to create exchanges that will satisfy individual and organization objectives.[2] Marketing is based on the fundamental element of exchange. *Exchange* is the process by which two or more parties give something of value to each other to satisfy each party's perceived needs.[3] The exchange culminates the marketing effort, but it actually has many preceding steps.

Although you may think marketing comes into play only when products are ready to be sold, marketing actually begins with the design of products. Firms conduct marketing research to determine consumer preferences for products; and marketers incorporate these preferences into product style, color, shape, durability, safety, and many other concrete decisions. Packaging styles and material decisions, for example, are influenced by findings from marketing research efforts.

Other marketing-related activities include pricing and distribution strategies. For example, marketing managers decide whether to price their brands at a competitive level or either lower or higher than prices for competing brands. The latter strategy, pricing above competition, is sometimes chosen so that the price might signal to customers an image of superior quality. Also, distribution strategy—the totality of physical distribution and the arrangement of channel members by which firms get their products to their customers—is an important marketing decision. Consider that Ralph Lauren clothes can be purchased in fine department stores, clothing boutiques, and manufacturer-owned shops. To preserve the line's reputation for quality, the company carefully selects what types of stores are qualified to carry the clothing line.

Advertising and personal selling—along with public relations, direct marketing, and sales promotions—comprise the communications aspect of marketing. Marketing communication involves selecting appropriate message and media strategies that target customers and achieve marketing objectives within budget constraints. Typically, persuasive marketing communication efforts cannot make up for a deficient product; but the combination of good product design and quality, along with effective advertising and other communication efforts, can substantially increase product sales, market share, and profitability.

Evolution of the Field

The sophisticated process that we know as marketing has changed greatly over the years. In earlier times, and sometimes even today, businesses emphasized manufacturing efficiency and devoted relatively little consideration to meeting customers' needs. This phase of marketing was known as the *production era*. Some businesses experienced the luxury of having customer demand exceed supply for their products; such firms stressed increasing production and reducing costs. This situation, called a *seller's market*, is virtually a relic of the past for most product-market situations in the United States and in other highly developed economies throughout the world. By the 1930s, technology had increased to the point at which firms in the United States could rapidly produce mass quantities, and demand no longer exceeded supply, thus ushering in a *buyer's market*. Firms realized that they had to increase sales in order to increase profit levels. Thus, aggressive selling, often with little regard for customers' needs, became the norm for the *sales era*.

Modern marketing in the United States came about roughly in the 1950s when firms realized that they needed to satisfy customers' needs better than their competitors rather than simply push onto consumers those products their firms were best able to produce. The *marketing era* and its inherent marketing orientation emphasize fulfillment of customer needs and customer satisfaction. This modern marketing philosophy entails coordinated efforts within a firm to meet customer needs while seeking long-term profits. Organization-wide coordination of efforts ensures that everyone in the firm will work together to satisfy customers profitably. Hence, the key theme in the modern marketing organization is one of designing and delivering products and services that fulfill customers' needs or wants and doing so in a way that provides the learning-adaptive marketing organization with a long-term sustainable competitive advantage.

WHAT TYPES OF MARKETING JOBS ARE AVAILABLE?

Marketing is so pervasive that you will find some type of marketing in every business, service organization, and not-for-profit institution. Indeed, employment prospects in marketing are plentiful. The majority of entry-level positions in marketing are in sales positions. Retailing jobs in a buying/merchandising capacity are also abundant. Remaining opportunities for entry-level marketing jobs include customer service, advertising, product/brand management, distribution, marketing research, and purchasing. A brief discussion of each of these areas should give you a better understanding of the types of careers available to a marketing major.[4]

Customer Service

Practically all organizations have some form of customer service because of the importance of customer satisfaction and repeat sales. Typical customer service responsibilities might include installing products, tracking shipments, answering questions, and following up on problems. This area is a good foot-in-the-door for college graduates because it offers them the chance to learn a great deal about a company's products and customers. Some companies hire customer service employees and move them into other areas after this initial job experience.

Advertising

Advertising jobs may be found in advertising agencies, in the many companies that advertise their goods and services, in the media (television, radio, newspapers, magazines, outdoor, and others), and with vendors that service advertising agencies (photographers, printing companies, graphic artists, and so on). Excellent oral and written communication skills are a must in the advertising world, as are problem-solving skills and a task orientation.

Positions commonly found in advertising include account executives who function as the liaison between an agency and its clients. Account executives develop creative strategies and assess the success of advertising. Media buyers and planners determine the media most appropriate for each client. They select the number of ads to be placed, appropriate media (such as TV or magazines), and suitable media vehicles (such as *Sports Illustrated* or *Newsweek*). They also coordinate placement and negotiate all media buys. Traffic managers see that the agency's work gets completed on time and are generally responsible for the larger, more involved projects. The creative staff produces the ads. Jobs in this area include copywriters, photographers, illustrators, graphic designers, and print and broadcast production people.

Brand and Product Management

Brand and product management is a key area in large consumer goods companies like Procter and Gamble or Coca-Cola. It is also a major function in business-to-business firms that market their products primarily to other businesses. Product and brand managers handle the marketing efforts for the brand(s) or product lines to which they are assigned. For example, the manager of Diet Coke is responsible for seeing that the brand meets its market and profit objectives and initiates marketing programs—advertising and sales promotion programs, packaging strategies, and so on—that will accomplish these goals. Because these positions are challenging and prestigious, such positions typically are reserved for individuals who hold MBAs from elite graduate schools of business.

Buyers/Merchandisers

Buyers and merchandisers are found in the retailing field. These positions include selecting items and brands to be sold by stores and developing an appealing array of products that will bring customers. Entry-level jobs include assistant merchandisers and area sales managers. Job advancement can be fast and quite rewarding for the individual who is successful in the early part of his or her career.

Distribution

Someone working in distribution might dispatch drivers, coordinate pick-ups and deliveries, oversee a warehouse, or manage materials. Opportunities depend upon the structure of the company; those companies who do their own transporting and storing will have more positions than a firm that hires out such tasks.

Marketing Research

Marketing research is generally seen as the most technical of all marketing careers. Market researchers must have strong analytical skills, an eye for details, and an ability to think conceptually and implement plans well. Market research is conducted by the specialized staffs of individual businesses and by specialists in marketing research agencies. Market researchers help define problems to be researched, develop tools with which to collect data, analyze findings, and recommend solutions based on the results. New college graduates might start as assistant research analysts and can expect to perform such tasks as questionnaire design, data analysis, interpretation of results, and report generation.

Purchasing

Larger companies, hospitals, governmental offices, and educational institutions have a need for a specialized purchasing agent or staff. Such jobs include identifying product and service needs, selecting the best source of supply, establishing purchasing criteria, and ensuring that levels of product quality are maintained.

Direct Marketing

Direct marketing is a rapidly-growing area. Direct marketers perform such duties as developing and maintaining databases, tracking responses, writing direct-mail pieces, and brokering lists.

Personal Selling and Sales Management

No discussion of marketing positions is complete without commentary on the role of personal selling and sales management. Sales positions comprise the vast majority of marketing jobs, and most entry-level positions include selling. You are probably familiar with retail sales clerks and those pesky telemarketers who want to offer another no-fee, low-interest-rate credit card. However, you may not know about the many other types of sales positions—like stockbroker, pharmaceutical detailer, hotel and convention planning sales representative, and industrial sales representative. A sales position with a large, sophisticated consumer-goods company or business-to-business firm can offer the college graduate abundant opportunities for professional and personal development and can lead to job advancement opportunities. Most salespeople are assigned territories in which they establish or maintain customer accounts. Successful salespeople have several options, including staying in sales, becoming sales managers, or moving into other marketing management positions. Most sophisticated firms today hire salespeople with the intent of directing their careers into various levels of sales and marketing management.

PREPARING FOR A CAREER IN MARKETING

Since there are a variety of positions in the field of marketing, no single educational path will ensure success. However, all competent marketing practitioners demonstrate certain core qualities. Good written and oral communication skills are a must. Analytical skills also are essential, as are problem-solving abilities. For example, modern salespeople do not push products on customers; they solve customers' problems. Hence, successful salespeople, as well as marketing practitioners, are effective problem solvers.

Undergraduate Education

The marketing degree is a business degree, so it will include courses that will develop your communication, analytical, and quantitative skills. Beyond that, the marketing program area offers a variety of courses to prepare you for different jobs. A Bachelor of Science degree in Marketing from a typical school of business requires students to take courses studying the principles of marketing, consumer behavior, marketing research techniques, and marketing strategy and planning. Additionally, a variety of electives can guide you toward a marketing career. Many colleges offer courses in marketing communications and strategy, marketing channels and distribution, personal selling and sales management, product management, business-to-business marketing, and services marketing.

Work Experience

Any applicable outside work experience you gain during your education may benefit you when looking for a career. Since many companies prefer to hire from within, you may have a better chance of being hired if you've already proven yourself to the business by part-time or summer work. Participating in an internship is another valuable way to learn more about different marketing jobs and can offer the same advantage as part-time work experience. Understanding that you may be able to earn more in other part-time work (such as construction or waiting tables), you should nonetheless consider how you can incorporate your work experience into your marketing education. Also, since you'll soon be marketing yourself to job recruiters, now is the time to begin preparing for future opportunities.

Student Organizations

When prospective employers evaluate candidates for marketing jobs, they consider academic performance, job experience, evidence of leadership ability, and various personal characteristics. In addition to performing well academically and acquiring meaningful job experiences, marketing students serve their interests well by joining organizations and assuming leadership positions. In addition to the various social and fraternal organizations that you may join on your campus, find out if your college has a student chapter of the American Marketing Association (AMA) or Sales and Marketing Executives (SME). Membership in a collegiate AMA or SME chapter provides an opportunity both to practice marketing (of the organization) and to learn more about the field of marketing in a non-classroom setting. All marketing students should seriously consider joining the AMA.

In addition, some colleges offer honors-type programs to a small number of outstanding marketing students. For example, at the University of South Carolina, top marketing students are invited to participate in the Marketing Scholars Program. This program affords an opportunity to work on a one-to-one basis with marketing faculty members and to learn more about issues of academic and practical import. If your college offers honors classes or clubs, you should aspire to achieve the grade-point average that will lead to being invited to participate in those prestigious programs.

INTEGRATION AND TRANSITION

Marketing is the third functional business area highlighted in the Business Function Integration model. This chapter has emphasized the breadth of marketing operations in U.S. business and the exciting range of career opportunities within this functional area. The chapter has also emphasized the dependence of marketing on the many areas of knowledge emphasized in the Recurring Themes model and its integration with other business functions, such as management (Chapter 7), operations (Chapter 8), and finance, which will be presented in Chapter 10.

As you can see, a successful business is one that is integrated and coordinates knowledge and skills from many sources and many individuals. Although your primary interest may be in one area of business, such as marketing, your career success will depend on your ability to view your organization and its needs as a whole, rather than as a set of separate, competing units.

Discussion and Action

1. What is *marketing*?
2. Describe how marketing applies to two radically different organizations, such as a neighborhood grocery store and an international company like PepsiCo.
3. Select a product you purchased recently. Identify marketing functions that were required to get the product to you. Identify marketing functions you performed in purchasing the product.
4. Which of the areas within the marketing discipline interest you as a possible career option? Why? If no area interests you, why is none interesting?
5. Identify ways in which the marketing function is dependent on the knowledge and skill areas shown in the Recurring Themes model.
6. Identify ways in which the marketing function is dependent on the other business functions shown in the Business Function Integration model.
7. Visit the Career Center on your campus. Find additional information about job opportunities for graduates with a marketing major. Be prepared to give a brief oral presentation (2–3 minutes) of your findings. Be selective as you prepare the presentation. Use the guides for business presentations given in Chapter 2.
8. Identify a businessperson who works in one of the marketing areas discussed in this chapter. Interview that person and report the results of the interview in a memorandum to your professor. Use the following questions to guide your interview.
   • When did you first become interested in this area? What stimulated your interest?
   • How long have you been in your current position? What previous marketing experience did you have? In what ways did that experience prepare you for this position?
   • Please describe a typical day in your position.
   • What advice would you give to a student who is considering a career in marketing?

Notes

[1]Adapted from John H. Lindgren, Jr. and Terence A. Shimp, *Marketing: An Interactive Learning System* (Fort Worth, TX: The Dryden Press, 1995).

[2]Peter D. Bennett, *Dictionary of Marketing Terms* (Chicago: American Marketing Association, 1988), p. 115.

[3] Lindgren, Jr. and Shimp. For further discussion on the theory of exchange, see Franklin S. Houston and Jules B. Gassenheimer, "Marketing and Exchange," *Journal of Marketing*, 51 (October, 1987), pp. 3–18.

[4]Material in this section was adapted from W. Glynn Mangold, *Marketing Careers, Marketing in Other Careers, and Marketing Your Career*, supplement to W. O. Bearden, T. N. Ingram, and R. W. LaForge, *Marketing Principles and Perspectives*, 2nd ed. (Boston: Irwin McGraw-Hill, 1998).

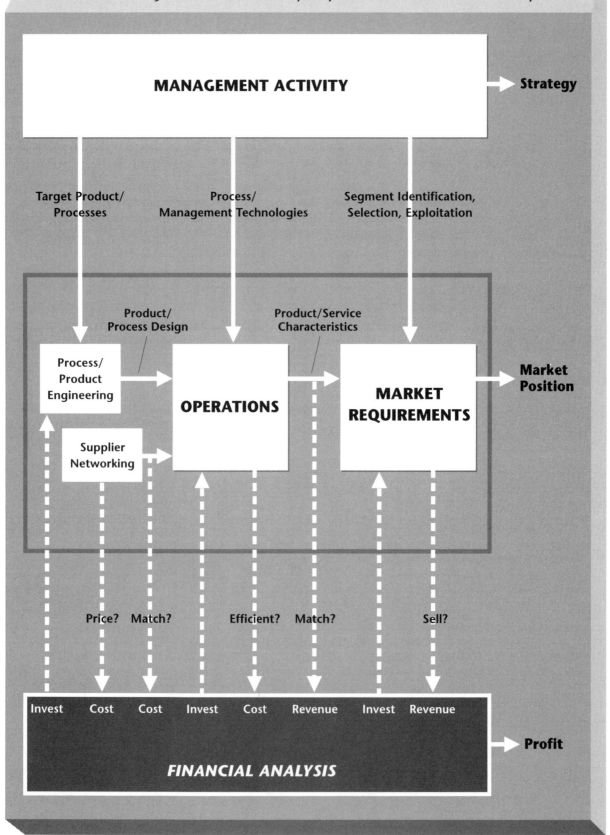

CHAPTER 10

FINANCE

OBJECTIVES

After you have read this chapter and completed related activities, you should be able to:

1. Identify ways in which finance influences your life.

2. Discuss why financial managers must be sensitive to many factors in the environment.

3. Identify sources of funds for businesses that need money.

4. Recognize the responsibilities and opportunities for a person who is interested in a career in finance.

Finance is part of our daily lives and is a critical element in determining our standard of living and quality of life. At the individual level, financial considerations often materially affect our choices of shelter, food, clothing, transportation, education, employment, associates, friends and entertainment. At the firm level, financial considerations often mark the difference between a profitable and a dysfunctional business, as is highlighted in the Business Function Integration model that precedes this chapter.

This chapter first introduces you to ways in which finance influences your life. Then it shows how effective financial practices can make the difference between a healthy and a sick company. Third, the chapter introduces you to capital and money markets as economic tools to make funds available to companies. Finally the chapter discusses responsibilities and opportunities for students who are interested in a career in finance.

FINANCE IN YOUR LIFE

We juggle financial and quality-of-life decisions whenever we make a purchase. If we pay too much for the better stereo system and then do not have enough money left over to buy the CDs that we really want, we are likely not maximizing our quality of life from the dollars available to spend. If we get the better stereo, buy the desired CDs, and then don't have enough money for food, we are still worse off. If we rent the better stereo, buy the desired CDs and have enough dollars for food, we may not have sufficient future dollars to eat or keep the stereo. Even if we have the future dollars to keep renting the stereo, we will be foregoing the use of those future dollars for other purchases and needs. Since the company renting you the stereo will only do so for a profit, you would clearly have less total consumption now and in the future by having the rental company "finance" ownership of your stereo. The choices on the use of your money are innumerable.

In the study of finance, a primary objective is to examine the possible alternatives before us on how we will consume and invest our limited number of dollars. Poor or rich, the question is the same: "How can we best use our limited money (or wealth) to maximize our current and future quality of life?" The quality of life that we speak of must be defined by individuals, and it differs from person to person. After at least maintaining a subsistence living, one person may want to use as much time and monetary wealth as possible in charitable contributions. Another person may want to use and store all remaining wealth for current and future needs of her or his children. Still another person may use the remaining wealth and extra time to earn still more money to buy a new expensive car for personal pleasure. The choices are yours. Finance decision-making tools can be used to define, evaluate, and make the final selection from the set of choices that most interest you.

In a private, free-enterprise economy individuals have a great deal of choice in defining their own best quality of life. In a controlled economy the state makes many of the choices for you about where wealth created from your productivity is spent. Your free will is restricted in determining how you will spend or invest the wealth created by your productivity. Even in a free society, the state has already determined to some extent the amount of your resources that will be allocated to defense, education, roads, welfare, safety, health, and so on. In both individual and company financial management we take as a given that we must pay taxes based on our society's decisions. Therefore, the primary objective of personal finance is to make sound financial decisions that maximize our wealth and lifestyle choices on what is left over after taxes. Finance techniques can also be used to increase our wealth by selecting available tax rules and differently taxed investments that legally minimize our taxes.

CORPORATE FINANCE

The study of corporate finance embodies a very similar objective to that of personal finance. The objective is for the corporation to make sound financial decisions that maximize the wealth of its investors. A corporation is a legal entity not limited to the life of its owners. In contrast, proprietorships and partnerships cease upon the death of an equity investor. Thus, a corporation provides ease of ownership change and continuance independent of its investors, while also enabling the easy and inexpensive transfer of ownership among investors. The added liquidity of the investor to be able to buy and sell the corporate investment quickly and inexpensively makes the corporate form of organization much more attractive than ownership in proprietorships or partnerships.

The Healthy Company

Rules and regulations from government agencies prescribe minimum society-determined standards on what the good "corporate citizen" must do in society's interests (see Chapter 3). Regulations cover everything from pollution standards, work safety standards, employer contributions to Social Security, product safety standards, truth in information provided to consumers, employees, and investors, and much, much more. To survive and be successful, the corporation must first satisfy society's standards. Further, the company must provide a competitive product to the market place (see Chapters 8 and 9 and the place of Operations and Marketing in the Business Function Integration model). If the quality of the product is below standard or the price of the product is above competitors' prices, the company will fail and investors will lose their wealth in the company. Thus, to provide a profit to investors, the company must first satisfy society's demands and then create a competitive product demanded by customers. The "greedy" corporate objective of wealth maximization for investors drives the existence of a socially conscientious company creating a quality product at a competitive price. Society wins, suppliers to the company win, employees win, customers win, and investors win. Only then has the company justified and enabled its continued existence.

Tools and techniques in corporate finance are used to define, evaluate, and make the final selection from the set of choices available to the corporation. For example, our company may need trucks to deliver its products. The evaluation of alternative trucks from different suppliers leads to a choice of the lowest-cost truck that has the required quality of service. This supports a purchase of a truck from the lowest-cost producer of a given quality truck and is consistent with supporting a competitive truck market. Our purchase supports the efficient producer and rejects the inefficient producer, thereby reinforcing competitive pressures to deliver a given quality truck at the best price. By satisfying its objective to make choices that maximize the wealth of our investors, our company also allocates funds to the most efficient producer. Simultaneously, we also lower our costs which in turn leads to both more taxes to satisfy societal needs and a lower cost of product to satisfy our customers. We gain a competitive advantage while also providing higher wealth gains for our investors. Again, everybody wins, except for the inefficient producers.

The Sick Company

Finance also considers the many ways companies can become dysfunctional and not satisfy the set of company *stakeholders* that include the society in which the company operates, suppliers, employees, customers, and investors. A dysfunctional, or sick, company generally has one stakeholder group that is too greedy and forces the company to favor it while the other stakeholders are forced to cover these extra costs.

Case Example One

If the employees enforce payment of excessive wages, the investors and possibly other stakeholders will not be adequately compensated for their contribution to the company. This type of problem could arise from managers paying themselves excessive salaries and having excessive perquisites (like private jets), or from employee unions demanding greater pay and benefits than can be supported in competitive companies. The company will be at a competitive disadvantage in attracting capital; it will cost more to get investor funds. The company must then charge a higher price for its product because of higher employee and capital costs, thereby becoming less competitive and less likely to survive in the long run. Everyone related to the dysfunctional company ultimately loses.

Case Example Two

Excessive government rules and regulations that impose greater costs than can be found in other nations also decreases the competitive advantage of companies relative to foreign companies that create the same product. This situation increases the likelihood that the company can only survive and prosper by moving to a foreign location where costs are lower and a competitive product price can be maintained. The society, local suppliers, and current employees lose.

A dilemma exists if the government-imposed costs include some required social benefit, like reduction of excessive pollutant emissions, while other governments do not have comparable pollution standards. Due to competitive objectives of delivering the best product at the lowest out-of-pocket cost, this type of problem transfers employment and wealth to the higher polluting country. For example, some people say that government-imposed costs have contributed to the transfer of production facilities from the U.S. to Mexico. This example of failure of a competitive system to work properly can only be resolved if acceptable world standards can be adopted and enforced. Failing to achieve this goal, the people of the world lose while consumers of the product pay less than would be required if uniformly acceptable pollution standards were enforced. Note that international standards can be achieved: Worldwide restrictions on the production and release of fluoro-hydrocarbons (used in air conditioners) that are thought to deplete the world's ozone layer have been adopted.

Case Example Three

Collectively, customers can also become greedy and demand more than a company can possibly deliver. There are no domestic U.S. private small aircraft manufacturers today. They were primarily driven out of existence by the costs of litigation. Nearly every time a small plane crashed, even if it was thirty years old, was flying in heavy fog, and crashed due to pilot error, the aircraft manufacturer was sued for faulty equipment. Because of the heavy litigation costs, investors could not foresee the possibility of getting an adequate rate of return on capital invested in these companies. Without capital, the companies failed. Small aircraft are still desired and would be purchased by many consumers if they were available. Everyone loses.

In each of these cases, the greed or excessive demands of one of the stakeholders ultimately results in the company's failure to compete effectively and survive in the long run. Thus, there is a delicate balance of contracts and agreements that is essential to a successful company's continued existence, and that must be appropriately renegotiated and changed for a sick company to survive.

CAPITAL AND MONEY MARKETS

The health of a company often depends on its access to funds. Corporations obtain money through the operations of capital and money markets. In those markets, investors make funds available by buying securities issued by corporations.

The Markets

The *capital market* enables the ready exchange of ownership rights to corporate and other market-traded securities. It is critical in supplying low-cost capital to corporations. Stocks and debt instruments with a maturity of more than one year are traded in the capital markets.

Since the cost of capital is a cost of production, reducing the cost also adds to society's and customers' quality-of-life enhancement. The issue of securities directly from the originating company to investors is referred to as the *primary market*. In the U.S. the New York Stock Exchange (NYSE), American Stock Exchange (AMEX), National Association of Security Dealers Automatic Quotation System (NASDAQ), and over-the-counter (OTC) markets are used to trade corporate bonds and stocks. This is referred to as the *secondary market*, because trading is in securities previously issued by corporations. A sound and efficient secondary market is essential in enabling investors to buy and sell securities quickly and with low transactions costs. The secondary market provides essential follow-up and continued trading of the securities directly issued to investors in the primary market and thereby reduces the cost of funds to a company.

The *money market* contains debt instruments with a maturity of less than one year. These are typically the safest investments. First, debt holders have a safer investment because they receive their promised principal and interest at maturity on the obligation before any funds can be paid to equity investors. Second, because their promised receipt will be within one year, unexpected changes in inflation or required interest rates have less impact on the value of the money market instruments than would occur with longer-term debt or equity investments. Thus, money market instruments are safe temporary investments that provide a modest rate of return to the investor. Corporations often invest in money market instruments with seasonal surplus cash funds that are not immediately needed for operation of the business. Investors use money market investments to store cash temporarily while determining where they will invest the available cash in capital market instruments.

Investments

An investor is willing to forego consumption today to achieve a higher level of consumption in the future. To effectively manage investments, the investor or investment manager must have a thorough knowledge of the types and characteristics of securities found in both capital and money markets. The investor especially needs to be aware of the risks and possible rewards associated with holding different types of securities. Risk assessment and management are key concepts in investing. For example, the investor needs to understand why investing in short-term debt, all else being equal, is safer than investing in long-term debt and why holding an equal investment in ten stocks in a portfolio is almost always safer than having the entire investment in a single stock.

Portfolio management deals with the management of a group (portfolio) of securities that can include different capital and money market instruments. Effective portfolio management is achieved when the risks and possible rewards from holding the portfolio are understood and intentionally controlled to meet the needs of the investor. For example, a young investor saving for retirement can invest primarily in common stocks even though large changes in the value of the portfolio of stocks up or down can occur for several years. Common stocks, though having much more volatile prices and returns in the short run than debt securities, have historically provided materially greater long-term returns (including dividends and price increases) than debt securities. Alternatively, an elderly investor in retirement is much more likely to be dependent on receiving a steady and near-certain cash flow of principal and interest from her or his investments to cover required living costs. This investor would not be willing to accept the risk of large losses to a portfolio that could occur with common stock holdings. The investor would rather invest in debt instruments with maturities that match future cash needs. The portfolio strategy and holdings in both cases are quite different, but each best suits the need of the particular investor.

RESPONSIBILITIES AND OPPORTUNITIES WITH A CAREER IN FINANCE

Accepting responsibility for your choices and actions is essential in successfully managing your life. You are encouraged to make wise choices to achieve personal fulfillment and the quality of life you desire. Joining a business school indicates your current interest in pursuing a professional career in business. You will accept numerous responsibilities if you select finance as your professional business major. Numerous and sizable potential rewards will come with a successful fulfillment of those responsibilities.

Mastery of the Language

A major commitment must be made to learn an extensive and sometimes overwhelming vocabulary of general business terms, and specific definitions of words and terms used extensively in accounting, computer science, economics, information systems, international business, finance, operations management, marketing, and statistics. The typical finance professional works in teams with people from the other functional areas of business and must understand what they are saying when they use business terms. To make matters more difficult, the same term or word often can have different meanings in different functional areas and across different companies. This learning is ongoing throughout your career; it does not end at graduation.

A mastery of the definitions encountered throughout your undergraduate program will provide you with the initial vocabulary skills required in the business workplace. Because finance is very closely tied to and dependent on accounting information and the economic environment, a finance major needs to focus particular attention on the definitions and terms from these two areas as well as the terms from finance.

Knowledge of the Environment in Which Companies Operate

To survive and thrive in any environment, knowledge of the environment and the rules and conditions that govern actions in that environment are required. For the business management environment, specifically company financial management or investor portfolio management, you need to understand the government's rules and regulations that constrain the behavior of companies or portfolio securities. The economic conditions and non-government institutions that have direct and indirect impact on business activities also need to be understood and appropriately considered in any decision making by the business or portfolio manager. The impact of a business decision on a company's performance (the accounting income statement) and position (the accounting balance sheet) should be simulated to understand the economic consequences of the decision on the company or on the portfolio of an investor who holds that company's stock. Heavy reliance on accounting and economics information reflects the dependence of finance decisions on a thorough understanding of both of these fields of study.

An Understanding of Finance Theory and Concepts

An understanding of financial theory includes knowledge of economic principles that determine valuation of projects, companies, different types of securities, and portfolios of securities. It also involves an understanding of the rationale underlying variables that impact the valuation of those items. For example, what is the expected impact on the value of a project, company, or stock portfolio if the government increases the corporate income tax by five percent? Clearly, your decisions as a company financial manager or portfolio manager would be influenced by such a change. This information would be needed for the more important decisions on changes in financial management strategy required to appropriately respond to your changing environment. Models will be provided in the finance program to answer this type of question.

An Understanding and Ability to Use Financial Decision Models

A decision model to determine the average return and risk of a given portfolio of stocks is required before the investor or portfolio manager can determine if the return-risk profile of the portfolio matches the investor's needs. The financial project manager in a company needs to determine the investments, operating costs, and revenues of a project, and the timing of those items before making a formal analysis to see if the potential profitability of the project justifies the use of investors' capital. These are two examples of fairly complex models used in finance to aid a portfolio manager and a company project manager to make appropriate finance decisions. The graduating finance major will need to be comfortable with understanding and using these types of models.

Numerous models of these types will be presented to finance majors. The student will need to understand the rationale and underlying economic theory and rules used in the construction of the models, and not just memorize the mechanical steps required to solve the model. A slight change in the environment would render the mechanical memorization useless in a later decision. An understanding of the rationale and logic underlying the model will give the student the capacity to modify the model to accommodate the changed environment. The memorization approach is unacceptable if you hope to have a transferable and useable skill for your career.

INSURANCE AND RISK MANAGEMENT[1]

An important financial function in every firm is the management of risk, which includes insuring against losses. Today's business managers must operate in an increasingly complex, global environment that generates many risks. Some situations, such as those involving strategic decision making, have the prospect for either gains or losses. However, other forms of uncertainty involve only the potential for loss. These losses can threaten not only operational goals such as profitability and growth, but also the organization's very survival. Some examples include property and income losses, environmental liability losses, product liability losses, and even losses in international operations due to political unrest in a country where the organization does business. Therefore, the study of risk management and insurance is a discipline logically connected to finance.

Risk management and insurance majors learn to analyze and effectively manage risks faced by organizations and by individuals. The risk management process involves three basic functions:

1. Identification of pure risk-loss exposures and evaluation of their nature, frequency, severity, and potential impact on the organizations.
2. The planning and organizing of appropriate risk control and risk financing techniques to minimize potential losses.
3. Implementing the risk management plan, internally with top management and externally with loss control organizations, insurers, and other risk specialists.

A major in risk management and insurance provides students with a sound understanding of the basics of risk management. In addition, students learn about the insurance industry. There are job placement opportunities with a wide variety of organizations that need risk managers, as well as with many insurance companies that need specialists in such areas as marketing, management, finance, computer systems, and personnel. Many students increase their employment options by supplementing their major in risk management and insurance with additional courses in finance, management, marketing, or management information systems.

INTEGRATION AND TRANSITION

Communication skills, computer know-how, statistical knowledge, experience with business law and ethics, and international business knowledge and skills are essential for success in the financial sector. As the Recurring Themes Model has emphasized throughout this book, knowledge and skills in each of these areas are essential to any business degree holder.

As the Business Function Integration model shows, contributions of the finance function are of value only when finance is appropriately integrated with the rest of the organization. No one functional component of a business enterprise (including finance, accounting, information systems, operations, management, or marketing) can stand alone or guarantee the success of the business. Even financial institutions, like banks and brokerage houses, need state-of-the-art accounting and information systems, capable managers, appropriate marketing, and efficient operations to survive and be successful.

Irrespective of the major you select, it is essential that you attain a clear recognition that success in any field of business, and for any business, is dependent on the successful management of the cross-ties and interdependencies that exist among all of the functional areas of a business's operations.

View the functional areas as members of the corporate team. With any key player failing to coordinate activities with all other members of the team, errors and omissions in the management of the company will result, often with dire consequences.

DISCUSSION AND ACTION

1. What is the primary objective of personal finance? of corporate finance?

2. Describe how finance applies to two radically different organizations, such as a neighborhood grocery store and an international company like PepsiCo.

3. Identify a healthy company and a sick company that are reported on in the business section or the news section of your local newspaper. What information about financial operations appears in the news story? What distinguishes the healthy company from the sick company?

4. Identify ways in which the finance function is dependent on the knowledge and skill areas shown in the Recurring Themes model.

5. Identify ways in which the finance function is dependent on the other business functions shown in the Business Function Integration model.

6. Visit the Career Center on your campus. Find information about job opportunities for graduates with a finance major.

7. Which of the areas within the finance discipline interest you as a possible career option? Why? If no areas interest you, why do you not find them interesting? Be prepared to give a brief oral presentation (2–5 minutes) of your findings. Be selective as you prepare the presentation. Use the guides for business presentations presented in Chapter 2.

8. Identify a businessperson who works in an area of finance discussed in this chapter. Interview that person and report the results of the interview in a memorandum to your professor. Use the following questions to guide your interview.

   - When did you first become interested in this area? What stimulated your interest?

   - How long have you been in your current position? What previous financial experience did you have? In what ways did that experience prepare you for this position?

   - Please describe a typical day in your position.

   - What advice would you give to a student who is considering a career in finance?

NOTES

[1]The description of Insurance and Risk Management draws heavily on the pamphlet "Risk Management: An Essential Part of the Common Body of Knowledge for Business," American Risk and Insurance Association, 1990.

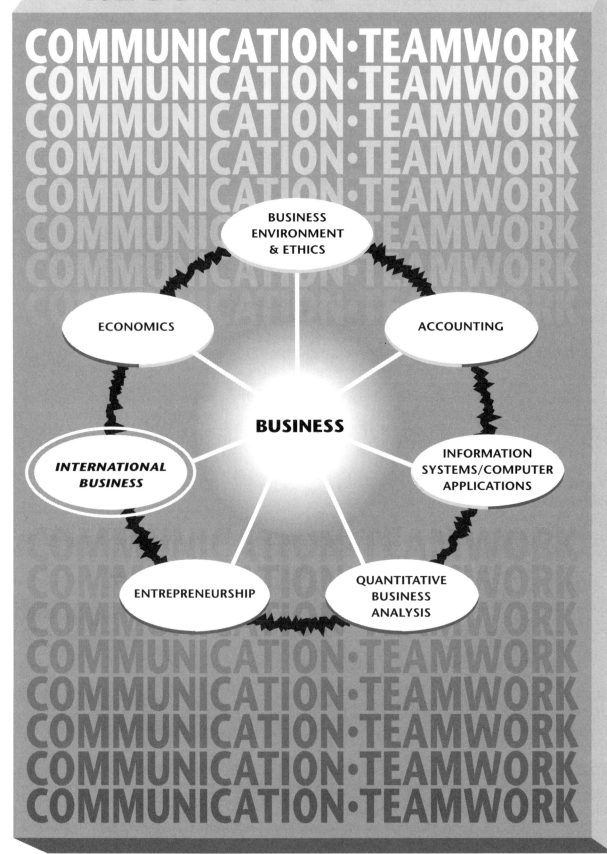

CHAPTER 11

INTERNATIONAL BUSINESS

OBJECTIVES

After you have read this chapter and completed related activities, you should be able to:

1. Recognize the breadth of international business activities and how they influence your life.

2. Identify where jobs in international business are most likely to be found.

3. Identify ways to prepare for a career in international business.

More than ever before, international business affects all of us—favorably, unfavorably, and occasionally both. As a result, it is increasingly important for everyone to understand how it affects his or her life and livelihood. In addition, there are increasing numbers of careers related to people suitably trained for these careers.

As you review the Recurring Themes model, you will see that international business is the final theme to be discussed. This chapter introduces you to the concept of international business and explains its extensive impact on your personal life and your career. Specifically, the chapter focuses on the importance of international business, where to find jobs in international business, and how to prepare for an international business career.

INTERNATIONAL BUSINESS: AN IMPORTANT FIELD

International business is all around us. It is the products we buy: imports, products made in this country by foreign-owned companies, and parts of products manufactured abroad that are assembled in this country. It is the places where we work, shop, bank, and vacation that are owned by foreign investors. It is Americans traveling abroad, and foreigners traveling in the United States. It affects the amount of money available for investment, lending, and borrowing, and the terms under which they are done, domestically and internationally. It affects the availability, variety, quality, and prices of most products and services offered domestically and internationally. Directly and indirectly, it affects the jobs, personal incomes, and standards of living of most people in this country and throughout the world.

In a very short time, there have been momentous changes in the world's political economy. What we knew as the Soviet Union, Yugoslavia, and Czechoslovakia no longer exist. The Warsaw Pact has been dissolved. Canada and the United States first enacted a trade agreement, which was subsequently extended to include Mexico, creating the North American Free Trade Agreement (NAFTA). The former European Community, now renamed the European Union, moved still closer to its goals of full economic and political integration, and Brazil, Argentina, Paraguay, and Uruguay established their own new regional economic block, MERCOSUR. Democracies and market-oriented economies were established in many countries that had not had them in decades, if ever, in their history. At least a dozen new countries were established, and new types of national leaders emerged around the world. New types of challenges have arisen, such as the global AIDS epidemic, global warming, and other ecological problems and concerns. The size and world rank of Japanese corporations reached an historic high, while that of U. S. corporations for the most part declined. China became one of the ten biggest economies in the world and the fastest-growing economy among the world's major economic powers. And world trade and investment continued to expand and diversify.

In essence, the global political economy has expanded and become even more dynamic than ever before. For virtually all countries, international business developments have an increasing impact on their national growth or survival. As a result, the demand continues to increase for academicians and business personnel who understand how the global economy works and how to work effectively in the global economy. While there were many opportunities for international business careers five years ago, today there are even greater opportunities, and this trend will continue into the future.

Although changes and new trends in the world affect international business, the activity of international business is centuries old. Not only is international business affected by changes, it has made its own contribution to cultural, political, and economic change throughout history. Nearly a thousand years B.C., ancient Phoenician sailors spread the products and ideas of the Near East, including an early alphabet, as far as what is now Britain and southern Africa. In the eleventh century, the expansion of trade and the resulting growth in the Western European economy led to the development of insurance, modern banking practices, and the reappearance of towns that had all but disappeared; this medieval international business also made possible the great cultural achievements of the Renaissance.

Modern international business has become so widespread and pervasive that it affects virtually everyone, everywhere. Every day of the year, some kind of international business takes place in the United States and throughout the world. If you type your research paper on a computer, drive a car, watch television, eat fruit, or play Nintendo, you probably have experienced the results of international business. Yet despite its importance, there remain many misconceptions about the definition of international business. Because of these misconceptions, most people do not understand how important it is, what opportunities it offers, or how their lives are affected by it.

Broadening Perceptions

People generally have only a vague idea of what international business actually is. To most people, international business involves only the world's largest corporations that build manufacturing facilities in other countries and sell products internationally. This is a very limited perception of who and what international business involves.

In broadest terms, international business is any business activity that occurs between people or organizations from different countries. In actual practice, there are many different kinds of international business carried on between different kinds of people and companies. For example, Americans traveling to a foreign country or foreigners traveling to the United States is international business. Americans purchasing a foreign-made product or foreigners purchasing a product made by an American company is international business. Shopping at a store in the United States owned by a foreign company or working in the United States for a company owned by a foreign firm is international business. Investing in a mutual fund that includes stock of foreign companies is also international business. These are only a few examples of different kinds of international business. However, this chapter emphasizes the two major kinds of international business in terms of volume, value, and importance. These two kinds are international trade and international investment.

International Trade

When a person or company in one country sells a product to someone or a company in another country, the transaction is called an *export*. If a person or company buys a product from someone or a company in another country, the transaction is called an *import*. Together, imports and exports comprise what is referred to as *international trade*.

In addition to products, services of various types can also be imported or exported. For example, if a U. S. citizen buys an airline ticket to Europe from a French airline company, the United States considers this a service import, and France considers it a service export. This example illustrates the dual nature of all international business transactions. What is an import viewed from one country's perspective is an export viewed from the other country's perspective.

Thousands of different products and services are exported and imported each year by the United States and other countries. One major category is raw materials, such as coal, tin, copper, rubber, and oil. Another major category is agricultural products, such as wheat, corn, soybeans, and cotton. A third major category is semifinished goods used in the production of other goods, such as computer chips, chemicals, seats and engines for automobiles, and fabrics for clothes. A fourth major category is finished products, such as transportation vehicles, computers, video recorders, televisions, shoes, and foods and beverages. The final major category is services, such as transportation services, consulting services, and financial services.

International Investment

If a company builds a manufacturing facility in another country, it is making a kind of international investment called a *direct investment*. Other kinds of direct investments include establishing in another country a sales office, warehousing facility, branch office, or some other kind of representative office; or buying land, commercial property (such as an office building or shopping centers), or a farm in another country. Direct investments also include joint ventures, collaborative investments made with another company.

If a company or person buys only a few shares of a foreign company's stock, or buys some government bonds of a foreign country, it is making a kind of international investment called an *indirect* or *portfolio investment*. Other forms of capital flows include making a loan to a person or company in another country or borrowing money from a person or company in another country.

The basic difference between direct and indirect investments is the intention of the investor. If the intent is to control the activities of the investment, it is a direct investment. If the intent is not to control, it is an indirect investment.

As is the case with international trade, international investment occurs in two directions. American companies such as IBM and General Motors build manufacturing facilities overseas, and foreign companies such as Toyota and Michelin build manufacturing facilities in the United States. American banks such as Chase Manhattan and Bank of America loan money to foreign companies and governments, and foreign banks such as Barclays and the Bank of Tokyo loan money to American companies and the U. S. government.

FINDING THE JOBS OF THE FUTURE

Under the broadest definition of international business, jobs will be available almost everywhere business is transacted. The basic reason is that international business trends will have an impact on most firms. As a result, they will need more employees who understand international trends, their causes, and their implications for the firms' future business strategies and activities.

In addition, more jobs will require people with an in-depth knowledge of international business and the very specific skills necessary to conduct business internationally. These kinds of jobs will involve working in an international context on a daily basis and are the types of jobs most commonly associated with international business.

Geographic Location

By definition and logic, most international business jobs will be increasingly available in the countries most heavily involved in international business. As a result, jobs will be most available in industrialized countries that are already major players in international business, such as the United States, Japan, Canada, Australia, and countries in Western Europe. In addition, international business jobs will be found increasingly in newly-industrialized countries such as China, Korea, Taiwan, Hong Kong, Singapore, Brazil, India, and Mexico. To a lesser extent, international business jobs will be found increasingly in other developing nations in the Pacific Rim, Latin America, the middle East, Eastern Europe, and Africa (probably in this order).

In virtually all cases, most international business jobs will be located in urban areas, and the biggest percentage of these jobs will be located in each country's largest cities. The reason for this is the larger metropolitan areas contain the largest number of firms and government agencies and also typically contain the country's biggest firms, which are most likely to be involved in international activities. Major urban areas also contain the greatest number of service facilities and industries that are likely to be involved in international business, such as seaports, airports, rail and truck depots, warehousing and distribution centers, international customs operations, and financial services firms.

Not all international business jobs will be located in major urban cities, however. Many companies involved in international business are headquartered in much smaller cities and some even in primarily rural areas. Examples include companies such as John Deere and Company in Moline, Illinois; Caterpillar Tractor Company in Peoria, Illinois; Dow Chemical in Midland, Michigan; Michelin Tire Company in Clermont-Ferrand, France; BASF in Ludwigshafen, West Germany; Volkswagen in Wolfsburg, West Germany; and Olivetti in Iverea, Italy. In addition, many multinational firms operate production facilities in small cities or towns or in primarily rural areas. Finally, smaller cities and towns do have smaller firms that are actively involved in international importing or exporting. Thus, while the greatest percentage of international business jobs will continue to be located in major cities, they will also continue to be available in other locations.

However, it is important to recognize that there is a difference between where international business jobs will be available and where you will be able to obtain them. The mere fact that a job is available does not mean that you will be able to get it. Many jobs will be restricted by law to citizens of that country. In addition, most companies prefer to hire citizens of the countries in which they are operating, even if there are no legal requirements to do so. Staffing operations in each country with citizens of that country is almost always less expensive. It is also politically wise in terms of making a favorable impression on the citizens and politicians of that country. In addition, non-native employees will not know as much about the country as employees who are citizens of the country. As a result, they may not be able to work as effectively or efficiently.

These distinctions are important because they underscore differences in the types of jobs in international business even at an identical location. As an example, consider the French subsidiary of a company headquartered in the United States. In the French subsidiary, virtually all of the employees will be French citizens. Most, if not all, of their primary responsibilities and activities will involve only the firm's operations in France. In a broad sense, they are working in international business because they are employed in a company owned by a foreign investor. However, most of them will not be conducting international business activities specifically unless they are also involved in importing or exporting.

In this same French subsidiary, however, there will probably be several employees who are citizens of the United States on temporary assignment from the parent company. These kinds of employees are called *expatriates* during the times they are working in one of their company's foreign subsidiaries. Expatriates are typically utilized when they possess certain skills or experience that are not sufficiently available in a foreign subsidiary. In addition, expatriates are also utilized by the headquarters company to exercise greater control over foreign subsidiaries and to facilitate the coordination of subsidiaries' plans and operations with those of the larger multinational firm. In these respects, expatriates are involved directly and specifically in international business activities. To conduct their responsibilities, they should be bilingual, bicultural, and familiar with business practices and their firm's operations in France and the United States, and possibly in other countries as well. Whatever unique characteristic expatriates possess, they must be beneficial enough to offset the typically lower costs of using local citizens and the benefits that local citizens bring to the subsidiary's operations.

In sum, in virtually all locations of international business there will be different types of jobs. Some jobs will be much more directly involved in international business activities, while others will be more involved with local operations. Because of the unique skills and advantages each group possesses, expatriates are most likely to be involved in more locally-oriented kinds of jobs. Therefore, where you work in international business is not just a question of the availability of international business jobs; it also is a question of your unique qualifications for different types of jobs. For example, depending on the specific skills they possess, German citizens can work in Germany for German-owned firms that do business internationally or work for foreign investors in Germany. They can also work abroad in foreign subsidiaries of German multinational firms or work abroad for non-German companies that do business in Germany or other German-speaking countries.

Industries

On a global basis, some industries are growing very rapidly in terms of international business activity while others are growing less rapidly. At the same time, some industries are not growing at all internationally while a few are actually declining in terms of international activity. In addition, due to shifts in international competitiveness, one country's industry may be declining in international business activity during a time when the same industry in another country is increasing its international activity. Therefore, international business jobs in any industry will be affected by how the industry is doing domestically and globally.

In terms of broad categories of industries, major global expansion is likely to continue at very high rates in electronics, telecommunications, pharmaceuticals, leisure products, and services, particularly financial and information services. Other industries likely to continue to experience good growth rates globally include chemicals, transportation vehicles and parts, health-related industries, tourism, and many consumer products, such as specialized foods and beverages, toiletries, and appliances. All these industries generally involve products that are tied closely to economic development, growth in per-capita income, and changing lifestyles. Slower growth can be expected for steel, forest products, textiles, apparel, many natural materials, and most fabricated metals.

Functional Areas

The fastest and biggest growth in international business jobs will probably occur in international finance and accounting. As international trade and investment continue to expand, international finance and accounting jobs will have to expand commensurately in order to obtain and manage money, to account for transactions, and to provide more accurate information on which to make a wide variety of business decisions. In all likelihood, these two areas also will continue to offer the greatest number of entry-level jobs in international business and the best opportunities for working abroad.

International purchasing and marketing are two other functional areas where more jobs are likely to exist in the future. In order to remain or become more competitive, more and more firms are purchasing raw materials, semi-finished products, technology, services, and equipment from foreign suppliers. International purchasing allows the firm to get what it needs at lower prices, better quality, and sometimes both; it may also allow the firm to obtain things it needs that are just not available locally. As more firms recognize these advantages of purchasing internationally, they will need more personnel who can do it well. Viewed from the other side, increased international purchasing creates increased demand for personnel who can sell a company's products or services internationally. It also requires employees who can identify potential customers in foreign markets and who can develop an appropriate strategy to make potential customers aware of the company's products or services and then convince them to buy them.

Another functional area where there will be more international business jobs in the future is international production. While many firms prefer to purchase what they need from foreign suppliers, there are often advantages for companies to produce by themselves what they could purchase. One major advantage is that the firm gains better control over costs, quality, and availability. It also does not have to share secretive or otherwise important information about the company with suppliers.

There is also a completely different situation in which international production may be needed or beneficial. A firm might not be able to export its product to a foreign country or may face limitations on how much it can export. In either case, one alternative is to establish production facilities in that foreign country, the output of which is sold entirely or primarily in that country.

International logistics is another area where there will be additional jobs in the future. Whenever international trade takes place, products must be physically moved from one country to another. This physical movement of goods involves collecting the goods to be shipped, arranging for their transportation out of the country and into the importing country, and ultimately delivering the goods to the customer's location in the other country. It may also involve arranging for the storage of the goods in the importing country until they can be delivered to the customer. All of this is international logistics, which must be done in a timely and secure manner. As international trade and investment increase, so will jobs in international logistics.

International planning and management are the final areas where jobs in international business will become increasingly available. Increasing international business of all forms will require more people who can plan and manage the international activities of their companies or their affiliates. In addition, there will be a need even in firms that do not have any international activities: These firms will increasingly need to have planners and managers who understand how international trends (such as import competition) may impact the companies' operations in their domestic market.

The Long-Term Prospects for International Business Jobs

The long-term prospects are highly favorable for jobs in international business. International business activities will be increasing steadily in amount and variety. More countries, industries, and companies will be involved, as well as more locations in each country. More jobs will be directly involved in international business or will have international aspects occasionally. More jobs will also be created in industries that support and facilitate international business activities. Finally, additional international business-related jobs will become available in the educational system because of the need to educate and prepare people for lives in an increasingly internationalized world.

However, it needs to be pointed out again that the existence of more international business jobs does not mean that you will be able to get one. You will have to be eligible, properly prepared, and have the appropriate motivational attributes.

PREPARING FOR AN INTERNATIONAL BUSINESS CAREER

There is no simple, magical method of preparing for a career in international business. Proper preparation is really a lifetime process involving many different steps and experiences beginning as early as childhood. Some take place in the formal educational system while others occur outside it. Some can be completed in your own country while others require an international setting. All of the steps and experiences are useful, and some are crucial; having more experiences is better than having fewer.

Cultural Experiences

One extremely valuable type of cultural experience is international travel. The more countries you visit, the broader will be your perspective. When visiting foreign countries, it is important to explore areas that are not on the normal tourist's itinerary in order to observe the real living and working conditions in the country. In general, it is much more educational to stay in lodgings and eat in restaurants that are not frequented almost entirely by tourists. Using public transportation whenever possible is also enlightening and relatively inexpensive. It is also beneficial to negotiate an informal tour of the city and countryside with a local taxi driver, asking the driver to show you some of the nontourist areas.

While the number of countries you visit is important, it is also important to spend an adequate amount of time in each country. Depth of experience is as important as breadth. A whirlwind tour of six countries in five days is not likely to be a very enlightening experience, other than learning why you would not want to do it again. Therefore the longer you can stay in a country, the more you will learn about things that will be really useful to you.

While one of the main benefits of international travel comes from interacting with foreign people, you do not have to travel internationally to have such interaction. Take advantage of the many opportunities to meet foreign people in your own country. Interacting with citizens from foreign countries who live, study, or work in your community is an excellent and relatively inexpensive way of learning about other cultures. Once you look for them, you will probably be surprised to find out how many citizens from other countries live in or visit your own community. For example, the owners and operators of many international restaurants are natives of the countries whose cuisine they feature.

Citizens of other countries can also often be found working in local firms owned by foreign investors. In addition, many cities have organizations, such as international visitor councils, that try to arrange meetings between foreign visitors and local inhabitants, including home visits and home stays. Some organizations arrange local housing for students from other countries, while others sponsor cultural events pertaining to foreign countries, such as German Oktoberfest or a French Bastille Day. At such events, chances are good that you can meet some citizens from the featured country in addition to being able to learn something about the country's culture.

In many cities there are organizations whose purpose is to bring together people interested in a particular country, such as the Alliance Francaise for France, the Goethe Institute for Germany, the U.S.–Korea Society, and the U.S.–Japan Society. Becoming affiliated with such organizations can be an excellent way to meet people and learn more about these countries. Finally, do not neglect opportunities to learn vicariously about other countries by seeing foreign films shown in your community. Chances are also good that you will be able to meet people from these countries at the movies.

Formal Education

The formal education system offers many opportunities for you to obtain the outlook, background, and operational skills necessary for a career in international business. Properly preparing yourself for such a career involves taking advantage of as many of these opportunities as early and frequently as possible. However, do not despair if you have already missed some of the possible opportunities. It is almost never too late to get started.

At the undergraduate level, opportunities abound for developing an international awareness, background, and outlook. Most good undergraduate programs offer a wide range of required and elective courses that are international in scope. Examples include courses about world history and the history of different regions or countries of the world, world geography, comparative political science, cultural anthropology, comparative religion, international economics, international business, foreign languages and literature, and many other courses about specific areas of the world (typically referred to as area studies courses). All of these courses are good preparation for a career in international business and provide the breadth of knowledge you will ultimately need in your international business career. They usually help you decide which geographic area of the world you are most interested in or suited for in terms of your future specialization.

While it is helpful to have already developed some foreign language ability before entering undergraduate school, it is very important to develop and enhance your foreign language ability during your undergraduate program regardless of your major. Ideally, you should take four years of language training in a specific foreign language. Foreign language courses focusing on business terminology are especially useful. Whenever the requirements for the degree you are pursuing permit options that include internationally-oriented courses, take every one you can. At the undergraduate level, breadth of exposure is generally better than depth.

Many undergraduate programs also offer opportunities to spend a semester or year abroad or have shorter-length, study-abroad programs. These opportunities are extremely valuable preparation for a career in international business, and you should take advantage of at least one. Even if your school does not offer these programs, many other schools offer such programs on an open enrollment basis. Study-abroad experiences permit you to continue your studies while being immersed in a foreign cultural setting, and are an excellent way to achieve multiple goals simultaneously.

Several majors at the undergraduate level are useful, but some are likely to be more useful than others. In addition, much depends on whether you plan to get a graduate degree. Generally speaking, the most useful major for a career in international business is not one specific major but a multidisciplinary major or a dual major with an international orientation. Examples include area studies such as European studies or Asian studies and dual majors in business and foreign languages, economics and international studies/political science, or any technical major (engineering, chemistry, or biology) with some other major that is international in focus. To most internationally-oriented companies, multidisciplinary degrees are considered better preparation and more desirable for international business careers than a degree in any single subject. They are also typically considered better preparation by most graduate programs in international business you may want to enter.

It is also desirable to take several courses in business at the undergraduate level, regardless of your major. The basic courses in business, such as accounting, management, operations, marketing, and finance will provide you with some understanding of business in general and which kind of job in business you are most interested in and suited for. In addition, many business schools offer special sections of these courses to non-business majors. If your degree requirements permit you to take only one business course, a course in business for nonbusiness majors is probably the best one to take. If such a course is not available, the first course in management is a good alternative because it typically provides a general overview of business.

Finally, it is important that you recognize that there still are not many entry-level jobs in international business, and there are even fewer for people with only undergraduate degrees. Most entry jobs in international business for persons with undergraduate degrees initially involve export or import documentation, language translation, international shipping, or tourism. There may be slightly higher-level jobs in smaller companies involved in, or planning to become involved in, international trade. Excellent preparation for these kinds of entry-level jobs is a degree that combines international business and some other international field, such as foreign languages or international studies.

INTEGRATION AND TRANSITION

A successful international firm draws from and applies all areas of knowledge diagrammed in the Recurring Themes model and in the Business Function Integration model. Such a firm draws information from its external and internal environments and communicates that information effectively across functions within the company as it plans and manages its domestic and international strategy for operations, marketing, and finance.

To be successful in the international and domestic business arena, you also must have a working knowledge of communication and teamwork, economics, the business environment and business ethics, accounting, information systems and computer applications, quantitative business analysis, entrepreneurship, and international business. As an effective employee, manager, or entrepreneur, you will use knowledge and skills in those general areas to effectively integrate the management, operations, marketing, and finance functions of your firm.

The contributors to this book wish you success as you pursue your specific business major and related areas of study and prepare yourself for *your* transition into business.

DISCUSSION AND ACTION

1. Define the following terms:
   - international business
   - imports
   - exports
   - direct international investment
   - indirect international investment
   - expatriates
2. Identify ways in which you were involved in or affected by international business within the past week.
3. Identify a recent political or economic event that has an impact on international business. What types of companies were most affected by that event? How has that event affected the way those companies do business?
4. In what geographic areas are you most likely to find a job in international business? In what industries?
5. What can you do during your college years to help you get a job in international business?
6. Explore opportunities on your campus or in your community to learn about the people and cultures of other countries. Present your results in a report to your professor. Use the report format described in Appendix E and include a title page, as illustrated in Appendix D. Your instructor will specify the approximate length of the report.
7. Visit the Career Center on your campus. Find information about international job opportunities either in a functional area that interests you or in a country that interests you. Report your findings in a brief presentation to your class.

REFERENCES

Much of this chapter is reprinted from *Opportunities in International Business Careers*, ©1995 by J. S. Arpan. Used with permission by NTC/Contemporary Publishing Group.

APPENDIXES

These appendixes demonstrate standard formats for business documents. The text of each document provides guides for its format. Please read the document and follow the guides as you write letters, memos, and reports for this course and other business courses. The appendixes also give forms to evaluate a business presentation and the behaviors of group members.

- *Appendix A.* Block Letter Format. The block format is the most widely used letter format in U. S. business.

- *Appendix B.* Simplified Block Letter Format. This is a useful format when you do not feel comfortable using the standard letter greeting, such as when you do not know the name or title of the individual to whom you are sending the letter.

- *Appendix C.* Standard Memorandum Format. The memorandum is widely used for written communication within an organization.

- *Appendix D.* Report Title Page.

- *Appendix E.* Single-spaced Report

- *Appendix F.* Double-spaced Report

- *Appendix G.* Levels of Headings in Reports

- *Appendix H.* Oral Presentation Evaluation

- *Appendix I.* Evaluation Guide—Group Behaviors

Appendix A. BLOCK LETTER FORMAT, OPEN PUNCTUATION

K&T Communications Consultants
K&T Communications Consultants
Suite 116, Castle Complex
1218 Barnwell Street   Telephone: 303-555-5974
Denver, CO 80202-1201   Fax: 303-555-5975

January 19, <year>

Ms. Maria Peters
Communications Director
Peters Fine Foods
1849 N. Halifax Avenue
Jacksonville, FL 32018-4421

Dear Ms. Peters

This letter demonstrates block letter format. The block format is used extensively in business today. Its efficiency and clean appearance are pleasing to contemporary business writers.

In block format, all lines begin at the left margin. No letter parts or paragraphs are indented. The letter is typed in single spacing, with double spacing between paragraphs. Right and left margins should be at least one inch wide. Space approximately four times between the date and the letter address and from the closing to your typewritten name. Place your written signature in the space above your typewritten name.

This letter also demonstrates open punctuation, with no punctuation marks after the greeting and the complimentary closing. Mixed punctuation, which has a colon after the greeting and a comma after the closing, may also be used.

I think you will find the block letter format useful for your business letters, Ms. Peters. If you have questions about other letter formats, I will be happy to discuss them with you and provide illustrations.

Sincerely

Shirley Kuiper, President

APPENDIX B. SIMPLIFIED BLOCK LETTER FORMAT

K&T Communications Consultants
K&T Communications Consultants
Suite 116, Castle Complex
1218 Barnwell Street   Telephone: 303-555-5974
Denver, CO 80202-1201   Fax: 303-555-5975

January 19, <year>

M. Peters
Communications Director
Peters Fine Foods
1849 N. Halifax Avenue
Dayton Beach, FL 32018-4421

SIMPLIFIED BLOCK LETTER FORMAT

This letter demonstrates the simplified block letter format.

- The format has the following features.
- Left and right margins are at least one inch wide.
- All lines begin at the left margin.
- A subject line replaces the traditional greeting. The subject line may be keyed in all capital letters or in upper- and lowercase letters. Double space before and after the subject line.
- The letter body is single spaced with double spacing between paragraphs.
- Major points may be bulleted or numbered, but such emphasis techniques should be used only when they complement the message content.
- The complimentary close is omitted. The writer' s name is placed on the fourth line below the letter body. The writer's title or department may be included. The signature block may be keyed in all capital letters or in upper- and lowercase.

Although the simplified block style may be used for any correspondence, it is especially useful when you do not know the courtesy title of your receiver. On such occasions, use no title in the inside address.

Many of our clients have adopted this format as a company standard. We think you will find it useful for correspondence at Peters Fine Foods.

martha W. Thomas

MARTHA W. THOMAS—VICE PRESIDENT

APPENDIX C. STANDARD MEMORANDUM FORMAT

To: *Transition* Students

From: Shirley Kuiper and Martha Thomas

Date: September 17, <year>

Subject: Standard Memorandum Format

This illustration demonstrates standard memorandum format. Please notice the following features of memo format.

1. The standard heading consists of the captions *To, From, Date,* and *Subject*. Those captions may be arranged in different ways, but either *Date* or *To* should be the first item, and *Subject* should immediately precede the memo body (message).

2. The subject line should be a brief statement that will help the reader identify the memo's content.

3. Left and right margins should be at least one inch wide.

4. The memo body is single-spaced. Use double spacing between the heading and the first paragraph of the body; also use double spacing between paragraphs.

5. Related items may be grouped and marked with numbers or bullet points to focus the reader's attention on specific information. Numbered items also permit a reader to identify specific items for response. Always use an introductory statement before a numbered or bulleted list to provide unity and coherence. If a memo contains only one major point, do not number it.

6. The memo sender frequently places her or his initials after the type-written name to indicate approval of the message. Some writers sign or initial the memo at the end of the message. However, do not use a closing line, such as "Sincerely" or "Yours truly," at the end of the memo.

Please follow these guides as you prepare memos for this course.

APPENDIX D. REPORT TITLE PAGE

Format for Manuscript Report

Prepared for

Mountain View Industries
13666 E. Bates Avenue
Aurora, CO 80014

Prepared by

K & T Communication Consultants
Suite 116, Castle Complex
1218 Barnwell Street
Denver, CO 80202

January 19, <year>

APPENDIX E. SINGLE-SPACED REPORT

Format For Single-Spaced Report

This illustration explains one commonly used format for business reports. Notice these features of the report format: title page, margins, typography, report headings, and spacing.

Title Page

A title page may be used to orient the reader to the report and its writer. The title page should include the report title, for whom it is written, by whom it is written, and the transmittal date. Optional items are the company logo and other design elements that suggest the report content or the nature of the organization.

Although a title page may be optional in some situations, a creative design can create a positive first impression. Therefore, choose a format that conveys your professionalism.

Margins

Place the title approximately 1-1/2 inches from the top of the first page of the report. Use a 1-inch top margin for all remaining pages. If the manuscript is unbound or stapled in the upper left corner, use a 1-inch left margin. For a left-bound manuscript, use a 1-1/2-inch left margin. Right and bottom margins should be approximately 1 inch on all pages.

Typography

Use a *serif* font (a font with extenders on the letters) for the report text. For variety, you may use a *sans-serif* font (a font with no extenders) for the report title and headings. Use no more than two typefaces in your report. This illustration, for example, uses a *sans-serif* font (Futura) for the headings and a *serif* font (Palatino) for the report text. It would also be appropriate to use the same typeface, preferably a *serif* font, for headings and report text.

Spacing

This single-spaced, blocked format is used extensively by contemporary business writers. All paragraphs are single spaced. Use triple or quadruple spacing after the title, with double spacing before and after headings and between paragraphs.

Since some readers prefer the double-spaced format shown in Appendix F, always determine reader preference before completing the final copy of your report.

Report Headings

Use headings in any report containing more than one major section. Headings should orient the reader to the report content.

Type style and placement must indicate the relationship of headings and subheadings. Notice that the headings in this report are centered and keyed in identical style. If subheadings were used in any section, they would be keyed and placed to distinguish them from the main headings. For example, subheadings might be placed at the margin. Use of subheadings is illustrated in Appendix G.

APPENDIX F. DOUBLE-SPACED REPORT

Format For Double-Spaced Report

This illustration explains the double-spaced format for business reports. Notice these features of the report format: title page, margins, typography, report headings, and spacing.

Title Page

A title page may be used to orient the reader to the report and its writer. The title page should include the report title, for whom it is written, by whom it is written, and the transmittal date. Optional items are the company logo and other design elements that suggest the report content or the nature of the organization.

Although a title page may be optional in some situations, a creative design can create a positive first impression. Therefore, choose a format that conveys your professionalism.

Margins

Place the title approximately 1-1/2 inches from the top of the first page of the report. Use a 1-inch top margin for all remaining pages. If the manuscript is unbound or stapled in the upper left corner, use a 1-inch left margin. For a left-bound manuscript, use a 1-1/2-inch left margin. Right and bottom margins should be approximately 1 inch on all pages.

Typography

Use a *serif* font (a font with extenders on the letters) for the report text. For variety, you may use a *sans-serif* font (a font with no extenders) for the report title and headings. Use no more than two typefaces in your report.

This illustration, for example, uses a *sans-serif* font (Futura) for the headings and a *serif* font (Palatino) for the report text. It would also be appropriate to use the same typeface, preferably a *serif* font, for headings and report text.

Spacing

Some managers prefer this double-spaced, indented-paragraph format for business reports, especially for report drafts. All paragraphs are double spaced. Use triple or quadruple spacing after the title, with standard double spacing (no extra lines) before and after headings and between paragraphs.

Since some readers prefer the single-spaced format shown in Appendix E, always determine reader preference before completing the final copy of your report.

Report Headings

Use headings in any report containing more than one major section. Headings should orient the reader to the report content. Type style and placement must indicate the relationship of headings and subheadings. Notice that the headings in this report are centered and keyed in identical style. If subheadings were used in any section, they would be keyed and placed to distinguish them from the main headings. For example, subheadings might be placed at the margin. The use of subheadings is illustrated in Appendix G.

APPENDIX G. LEVELS OF HEADINGS IN REPORTS

Title	**EVALUATING EFFECTIVENESS OF VOLUNTEER ORGANIZATIONS**
First-Level	Determining Criteria for Effectiveness
	Xxxxxxxxxxxx xxx xxxxxxxxxxx xxxxx xxxxx xxxxxx. Xxxxx xxxxxxxxxx xxxx.xxxxx xxxx. Xxxxxxxxxxxxx. . .
First-Level	Assessing Effectiveness
	Xxxxxxxxxxxx xxxxxxxxxx xxxxxxx. Xxxxxxxx xxxx xxxx. . .
Second-Level	Setting Standards
	Xxxx xxxxxxx xxxxxxxxxx xxxxxxxx xxxxxxxx xxxxxxxxxx xxxxx. Xxxxxxxxx xxxxxx xxx xx xxxxx xxx. . .
Second-Level	Selecting Indicators
	Xxxxxxxxxxxxx xxxxxx xx xxxxxxx xxx xxxx xxx xxxxxxxxx xx xxxxxxxx. Xxxx xxxx xxxxxxxxxx xxxxxx x xxx xxxxx xxx. . .
Third-Level	Outcomes. Xxxxxxxxxx xxxx xxxx xxxxx xx. Xxxxxxx xxxxx xxxxxx xxx xxx. . .
Third-Level	Processes. Xxxxx xxxxxxxxx xx xxxxx xxx xxxx. Xxxxxxxxx xxx xxxxx xxx xxxxxxxx. . .
Third-Level	Structures. Xxxxxxx xxx xxxxxxxxx xxx xxxx xxx. Xxxxxxxx xx xxxxx xxxxxxx xxxxxx. . .
Second-Level	Selecting Samples
	Xxxxxxxxxxxxxx xxxxx xxxx xxx. Xxxx xxx xxxxxx xxxxxxx xxxxx xxxx. . .
Second-Level	Applying Measurements
	Xxxxxxxx xxxxxx xx xxxxx xxxx. Xxxx xxx xxxxx xxxxx xxx. . .
First-Level	Explaining Effectiveness
	Xxxxxxxx xxxxxxxxxx xxxxx xxxxxxxx xxxxxxx xxxxxxxxxx xxxxxxxx xxxxxxxxx xxxx xxx xxxxx xxxxxxxxxx xxxxx. . .

APPENDIX H. ORAL PRESENTATION EVALUATION

Presenter _____   Group _____

Scoring Key: 3 = very good; 2.5 = acceptable; 2 = needs improvement; 1.5 needs much improvement

Content and Organization		**Delivery**

Content and Organization

Introduction

    Attention arousal ___
    Orientation and preview statement ___

Body

    Soundly planned ___
    Easy to follow ___
    Clear transitions and summaries ___
    Effective development of topic ___
    Clear supporting material ___
    Appropriate detail ___

Conclusion

    Adequate summary ___
    Concise statement of
    recommendations, if any ___
    Placement of speech into
    larger perspective ___
    Effective closing statement ___

Presentation Aids

    Visible / readable / audible ___
    Aesthetically appealing ___
    Smoothly integrated into
    presentation ___

Delivery

Style

    Poise and confidence ___
    Awareness of audience;
    establishment of rapport ___
    Eye contact ___
    Freedom from reading ___
    Conversational tone ___
    Enthusiasm ___

Voice

    Enunciation ___
    Projection ___
    Pace ___
    Variety ___

Body

    Posture ___
    Movement & gestures ___
    Professional dress ___

Language

    Clear expression of ideas ___
    Correct grammar ___
    Avoidance of expressions
    peculiar to writing ___

Overall Effect

    Authoritative ___   Informative / Persuasive ___

APPENDIX I. EVALUATION GUIDE—GROUP BEHAVIORS

Instructions: List all group members, including yourself. Fill in the grid with codes to indicate the degree to which each person demonstrated the behaviors in a recent group meeting. F = frequently; O = occasionally; R = rarely; N (or blank) = never

BEHAVIORS	MEMBER NAMES							
Task-Oriented								
Initiates Discussion								
Seeks Information								
Gives Information								
Coordinates								
Evaluates								
Summarizes								
Process-Oriented								
Encourages								
Harmonizes								
Opens Gates								
Acts as Liaison								
Sets Standards								
Dysfunctional								
Blocks								
Seeks Recognition								
Competes								
Withdraws								
Repeats								